The American Townhouse

By Kevin D. Murphy

Photography by Radek Kurzaj

Abrams, New York

Concept Development, Project Management,
and Editing by Richard Olsen
Design by Judy Hudson
Copyediting by Sigi Nacson
Production Management by Jane Searle
Editorial Assistance by Isa Loundon

ISBN 978-1-4351-1994-0

Printed and bound in China
10 9 8 7 6 5 4 3 2 1

harry n. abrams, inc.
a subsidiary of La Martinière Groupe
Harry N. Abrams, Inc.
115 West 18th Steet
New York, NY 10011
www.hnabooks.com

Contents

Acknowledgments

The author would like to thank the following for their
assistance in researching and writing this book:

Michael Henry Adams
Jean-Christian Agid, French Embassy, New York City
Carrie Albee
Olivia Alison
Mark Benjamin
Rafaello Borello
Carroll Ann Bowers, Historic Charleston Foundation
Paul Bragaw
Corina M. Carusi, Glessner House Museum
Will Chandler
Flavia Cigliano, Nichols House Museum
Collin Clarke
Ulysses Dietz, Newark Museum
Wayne Donaldson
Richard Dudley
Margaret Halsey Gardiner, Merchants House Museum
Bryan Green
Beth Hannold
Kathy Hansen, National Parks Service
Anthea Hartig
Bernard Herman
Mickey Herr, Powel House
Shan Holt
James Jacobs
Tracey Link, Rancho Santa Fe Historical Society
Charles Lockwood
Jill Lord
Bridget Maley
Andrew H. Mann
Lorraine McConnell, Newark Museum
Katie and Joe Morford
Susan A. Nowicki
Julie and Wayne Padberg-White
Robert T. Parker, Mary McLeod Bethune Council House
Phyllis Paul
Martin J. Perschler
Jonathan Poston, Historic Charleston Foundation
Beth Richards, Elfreth's Alley Museum
Annie and Skip Robinson
Midge Rossini
Marty and Robert Rubin
Rima and Harlan Strauss
Grace Thaylor, Prescott House Museum
Barbara Thibault, Gibson House Museum
George Tonkin, Theodore Roosevelt Birthplace
Dell Upton
Susan and Paul Warren
Robert and Nancy Welcher
Nancy White
Richard Guy Wilson

*Circa-1840 houses lining Gramercy Park,
New York City. Photographed in 1934.*

The American Townhouse

"I wish Aunty Brownstone didn't love us so much!" opines a "Rural Child" to a "Mrs. Hayseed" in a humorous piece published in 1890 in the *Brooklyn Daily Eagle* newspaper. When pressed to explain her feeling, the child answers that "'Cause I asked why she didn't take us to the theatres, and parks, and parties, and such places w'en we visited her in th' city, an' she said it was 'cause she loved us so much she was *perfectly contented* to sit around home with us." So closely was the brownstone, a common sort of nine-teenth-century townhouse, associated with urban life and all of its pleasures, that the term could be used facetiously to denote an urban sophisticate whose ways were supposed to stand in sharp contrast with those of her country relations. Indeed, by the 1890s the townhouse defined the images of many estab-lished American cities in the popular imagination. However, on the heels of its nineteenth-century accept-ance as the norm for middle- and upper-class urban living, the townhouse was supplanted by the apart-ment as the city residence of choice for the affluent in the middle decades of the twentieth century, and the neighborhoods of houses in many American cities went into a period of decline. By the 1960s, the older townhouse and rowhouse neighborhoods of Amer-ican cities were revived and this was often directly tied to the renovation of the building stock. These neighborhoods provided the vibrant settings for plays, novels, works of visual art, and in the twentieth century, for television — for example, "The Cosby Show," which ran from 1984 until 1992. Bill Cosby's television family occupied a beautiful brownstone-fronted rowhouse in a neighborhood that recalled many of Brooklyn's gentrified residential areas.

Brooklyn, the independent municipality that became one of the five boroughs of New York City in 1898, is distinctive for its extensive and architecturally varied rowhouse neighborhoods. Before describing the history and variety of townhouses in Brooklyn and throughout the United States, it is necessary to define several terms. The term "townhouse" is com-monly used today in real estate advertisements to distinguish attached houses from freestanding residences. But in this book, the term is used more broadly, ranging from houses that are attached at both sides to their neighbors, to those that are free-standing but built close to the street and in rows of similarly scaled buildings. Within the category of townhouses is the subgroup of rowhouses. These are multistory houses, usually with narrow street and rear facades and longer fire-resistant, windowless walls at the sides shared with the adjoining residences. The characteristically long rectangular plan with exterior windows confined to the narrow front and back elevations, as well as the resulting dark core of the house, are features of rowhouse construction in the United States. The many rowhouses that were built in the nineteenth century, the heyday of their construction, were intended to serve as single-family residences, although large numbers were later divided into smaller apartments.

In rowhouse construction it became fashionable in the mid-nineteenth century to face the front eleva-tions with brown sandstone. The extensive construc-tion of these "brownstones" led to the widespread adoption of the term to describe any attached or semiattached urban house. It was in this sense that New York's Brownstone Revival Committee wrote in 1979 that, "Broadly, a New York brownstone is any rowhouse, brown or not, built before 1910 as a one-family home." In this book, "brownstone" will be reserved for buildings with actual stone facades and "rowhouse" will be used to denote a residence with party walls constructed as part of a group of similar buildings regardless of the material employed. The term "townhouse" will be employed to denote detached urban houses as well as large city houses which, although attached to one or more neighbor, nevertheless are conceived of as separate entities, that is, *not* as a component in a group of similar buildings.

This book illustrates the development of the townhouse from the time of earliest settlement of North America by English and European colonists through the twentieth century. In so doing, it will

Acorn Street, Beacon Hill, Boston, Massachusetts, with early nineteenth-century attached houses.

demonstrate the rise in popularity of townhouses in American domestic architecture which peaked in the late nineteenth and early twentieth centuries — when cities on both the east and west coasts and in the Midwest underwent periods of explosive growth. The decades of urban efflorescence were followed, after World War II, by years of rowhouse decline. As the examples of privately renovated houses included here demonstrate, urban decline was followed in the last several decades by coordinated efforts in many American cities to repopularize townhouse living and to bring blighted urban neighborhoods back to life. Some writers have speculated that the "brownstone revival" in New York City was spurred by rising apartment rents in the 1960s that made the ownership of an entire house more attractive.[1] Alexander Gorlin maintains that since townhouses are less than five stories in height, the maximum number which most people will climb, "It is therefore a housing type intimately related to the human size and scale."[2]

Whatever the motivations that lay behind its choice as a residential type, the townhouse first helped build and expand cities and by the eighteenth century was used to frame a residential square or park. In the later period of urban renewal, the twentieth century, the townhouse again played a decisive role, this time in the revitalization of city neighborhoods. Throughout the United States, former suburban residents rediscovered the pleasures of townhouse living. The home sections of newspapers throughout the country and "shelter" magazines regularly chronicle townhouse renovations and showcase their generally high-quality construction and appealing architectural features. Between the periods of urban growth and renewal, however, stretch decades in which the townhouse underwent numerous typological alterations as a result of changing concepts of the middle-class home and of domestic life more generally.

European Origins
The earliest American builders would have been familiar with European cities, where the close construction of houses had predominated for centuries. Indeed, classical Greek cities possessed blocks of densely packed houses, and in the city of Pompeii residential construction was typified by deep houses with narrow street facades. The centers of the Pompeian town houses — which needed illumina-

tion and ventilation — were often opened to the sky by atria. Elements of the Roman house plan would be favored by later builders. Following the collapse of the Roman Empire, the medieval period is often thought of as a time when sophisticated urban culture declined. Yet the fortified towns and cities of the Middle Ages were densely packed with houses. Historian Emmanuel Le Roy Ladurie has described how in the fourteenth century, in the southern French hill town of Montaillou, "stood the houses, one above the other, often adjoining, but sometimes separated by small gardens."[3] The development of what historian Fernand Braudel called "monster towns" extended from the end of the Middle Ages through the eighteenth century. Early Modern cities like Paris and London attracted huge populations and consequently suffered from environmental problems like shortages of space, light, and clean water. At the same time, these cities initiated new developments in the construction of adjacent or attached residences. English merchants of the sixteenth and seventeenth centuries built large houses that embodied characteristics of the townhouses of later centuries. The residence built by Thomas Prestwood in 1576, in Exeter, England, for example, typified merchant-house construction: It was around twenty to twenty-four feet wide and about 140 feet deep. At the street was a three-story block with a side entrance and at the center of the lot was an open courtyard. The rear of the site contained a smaller block consisting of the kitchen and other service areas. This typical plan echoed the arrangement of the Roman house while anticipating the later attached row ("terrace" in England) house.[4]

The rowhouse plan, with narrow-street frontage and a deep lot, as well as vertical circulation confined to a side hallway, was a response to increasing population density in the cities and larger towns of western Europe from the end of the Middle Ages through the eighteenth century. This trend in domestic architecture was accompanied by the use of rowhouses to frame open spaces that served a variety of purposes. For example, in the seventeenth and eighteenth centuries, in the city of Arras, in northeastern France, two large squares — the Grand' Place and the Place des Héros — were lined with similar looking tall and narrow houses in the Flemish Baroque style. Like the facades of the attached houses of Amsterdam, those that line the squares in Arras culminate in stepped or curved gables. At the ground story, however, the facades were opened for pedestrian traffic with continuous arcades based on Italian models. The walkways allowed for circulation between the commercial spaces that occupied the ground levels of the houses.

A similar formula was used in the development of a series of residential squares in Paris, each of which was intended — through the unified appearance of the houses that comprised it — to assert the authority of the king. In 1605 construction began on the Place des Vosges in the Marais section of Paris at the behest of King Henri IV. Originally, a silk works occupied the north range of the residential square and houses for silk artisans and merchants were constructed around it. As in Arras, at the Place des Vosges, ground-story commercial spaces were arcaded and the residences were located above. Inaugurated in 1612 as the Place Royale, the square made the point that the king was capable of creating order in the city.[5]

The Parisian Place Dauphine, dedicated to the future King Louis XIII, the Dauphin, followed the Place des Vosges in 1607. Like the Place des Vosges it was comprised of attached brick houses with white stone details, although the buildings have been largely altered in subsequent centuries. Among the later residential squares of Paris, which explored the variety of geometric forms that could be used to create an image of urban coherence, was the Place des Victoires, designed by architect Jules Hardouin-Mansart in 1685 to commemorate the victory of King Louis XIV at Nimègues in 1678. A statue of the victorious king (destroyed during the Revolution) at the center of the circular space connected military triumph with the ability to create order. The point made in these and later projects in Paris was the prestige that resulted from the sameness and coordination of facades, in contrast to the heterodox appearance of houses elsewhere in the city. The pattern established in these seventeenth-century projects would be taken up again

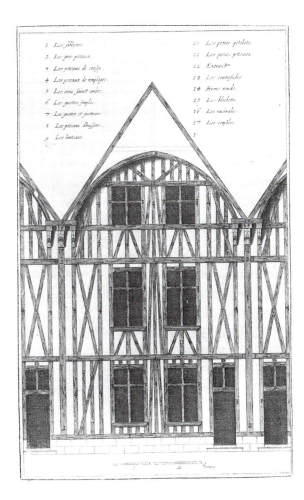

Place des Vosges, Paris, France, begun 1605.

Timber framing, from Pierre Le Muet, Maniere de Bastir pour Touttes Sortes de Personnes *(Paris, 1623).*

Place des Vosges, Paris.

in Great Britain and North America in the eighteenth and nineteenth centuries, until the idea of sameness lost its prestigious associations under the pressure of bourgeois individualism.

Similar developments occurred in London beginning in the seventeenth century. At the behest of King Charles I, and with the assistance of neoclassicist architect Inigo Jones, the Earl of Bedford developed a piazza at Covent Garden in London after 1630 with attached houses lining two sides. The houses, which have been destroyed, demonstrated Jones's familiarity with Italian neoclassical architecture and were connected by a first-story arcade as in the French projects described above. King Charles played a decisive role in the development of other groups of attached houses with neoclassical details, for instance in Great Queen Street and in Lincoln's Inn Fields. The former development, as architectural historian John Summerson points out, was particularly decisive in demonstrating the aesthetic value of uniformity in the city. "The Great Queen Street houses," writes Summerson, "were reputed in the eighteenth century, to constitute 'the first regular street in London'. They laid down the canon of street

design which put an end to gabled individualism, and provided a discipline for London's streets which was accepted for more than two hundred years."[6]

The Great Fire of London in September 1666 destroyed four-fifths of the city and provided a unique opportunity to rebuild and to create greater regularity among the houses. The Act for the Rebuilding of the City of London (1667) standardized house design and construction and established four classes of residences. The regulations created a hierarchy of houses, differentiated by numbers of stories and elaborateness of detailing, but insisted on certain commonalities like masonry construction. Post-fire London offered many opportunities for speculative building, especially of houses. Entrepreneurial builders popularized a townhouse, two rooms deep and with the circulation to the side. It has been hypothesized that Dutch houses from the seventeenth and early eighteenth centuries had established the common plan of houses one room wide and two or more rooms deep with a side passage. The sameness among London houses that emerged from the adoption of this prototype was enhanced by later regulations, especially the Building Act of 1774, written

Royal Circus, Bath, England, 1754. John Wood I, Architect.

by architects Sir Robert Taylor and George Dance, which codified four "rates" of townhouses and almost entirely prohibited the use of exterior ornament. Such regulations created an overall uniformity in the rapidly expanding city. The need to regulate building is understandable when considering that the population of London grew by nearly fifty percent between 1750 and 1800 to about 900,000 people. Some of the common features of the Georgian townhouse, including the use of red brick relieved with neoclassical stone or white-painted details, would have an important impact on American house construction.

The objective of giving the city a more coherent form by constructing visually unified townhouses around a park with a distinctive and geometrically pure form was realized most dramatically in Bath, England. The two architects responsible for the city's eighteenth-century transformation were a father-and-son pair, both named John Wood. The elder, who referred to himself as "the Restorer of Bath," gave the city what he saw as its appropriately classical architectural character — given that its hot springs had first been exploited during the Roman imperial period — by designing the Royal Circus,

a group of attached houses on a circular plan begun in 1754. The plan, as well as the use of the Doric, Ionic, and Corinthian orders on the facades, was directly borrowed from the Colosseum in Rome. The Royal Crescent, dating from around 1767 to 1775, was the design of the younger John Wood and followed his father's urban model by framing an area of greenery with a screen of townhouses treated as a unified composition. Here the thirty attached houses were detailed with engaged Ionic columns in the upper two stories. The Woods' projects address the potentially disturbing disorder and oppressive density of the British city of the early industrial age (although Bath was not industrial, it was notoriously crowded) with carefully arranged vestiges of nature surrounded by harmonious buildings. As Richard Sennett summarizes, "[T]he crescent form and the terrace house became staples of the English urban vocabulary, and these forms were thought, even more, as binding and unifying elements in the creation of a city."[7]

A project by the Scottish architects Robert and James Adam, who are widely credited with having popularized in the British Isles the neoclassical idiom

Hanover Terrace, Regent's Park, London, engraving 1827. John Nash, Architect.

associated with the Renaissance Italian architect Andrea Palladio, pursued the design of a block of residences as a grand composition — rather than just as a series of identical elements — in their Adelphi Terraces in London of 1768 to 1774. The group of twenty-four first-rate houses was one of the first in which the facades were treated as a single visual entity, like a long palace facade. The Adams' Palladianism in general, and their conception of the townhouse in particular, would have an important impact on American cities in the early nineteenth century.

Edinburgh was one of a number of cities in Great Britain that grew rapidly during the eighteenth and nineteenth centuries as a result of industrialization. Nearby Glasgow became the "Second City" of the empire on the strength of its tobacco trade and cotton manufacturing. Its population soared from 66,000 in 1791 to more than 200,000 in 1831. In both Glasgow and Edinburgh, growing middle-class populations were accommodated in terrace houses of varying sizes and degrees of elaborateness. Glasgow's most famous nineteenth-century architect, Alexander "Greek" Thomson translated the concept of the visually harmonious group of terrace houses into the Greek Revival idiom. He designed not only attached

houses, but also tenements — groups of adjoining houses that were divided into apartments for rental. Thomson thereby demonstrated that the concept of a unified row could be applied to housing at a variety of economic levels. Elsewhere in Great Britain and the United States during the nineteenth century, rowhouses were built in a wide variety of sizes to accommodate working-class and wealthier residents.

Thomson's contribution to adapting the Greek Revival style of the mid-nineteenth century to varieties of rowhouses had numerous parallels in London terraces. The project of framing a view of nature within the dense space of the nineteenth-century city is epitomized by Regent's Park in London, designed by architect John Nash for the Prince Regent, later King George IV, around 1813. The development included villages of detached houses as well as attached residences. The park was surrounded by glistening white terrace houses with bold Greek detailing, the construction of which continued into the 1820s. Nash's theatrical architecture has been the subject of criticism since the time of its completion. The Irish writer Maria Edgeworth commented at the time of construction that she was, "properly surprised by the new town that has been built in

Regent's Park — and indignant at the plaster statues and horrid, useless domes and pediments crowded with mock sculpture figures which damp and smoke must destroy in a season or two." Such dire predictions notwithstanding, the terraces constructed in the vicinity of Regent's Park endured to serve as examples of how groups of attached houses might be used to create impressive spaces within an expanding industrial city. Furthermore, the Greek-inspired detailing that Edgeworth lambasted was an indication of a stylistic transition from the restrained Palladian neoclassicism of the Georgian townhouse to a more sculptural and sometimes more archaeological idiom inspired by the architecture of classical Greece.

American Beginnings

Recent archaeological excavations at Jamestown, Virginia, the site of the first permanent settlement in British North America, have yielded evidence of a "rowhouse-style structure." The archaeological remains document the presence on Jamestown Island in the early seventeenth century of a house at least 150 feet in length that was a landmark of James Fort. What may have been the earliest group of rowhouses in Philadelphia, the so-called Budd's Long Row constructed around 1691 between Walnut and Dock streets, apparently drew on London pre-fire models. The group of ten houses, now lost, according to a nineteenth-century description by John F. Watson in *Annals of Philadelphia* (1830), were constructed of "heavy timber and filled with bricks" in a medieval manner.

While the internal arrangements of some of the early rowhouses are not yet fully understood, architectural historian Bernard Herman has identified the presence in early America of a number of types of attached houses, some with relationships to English precedents. One of these, familiar from the London rebuilding after 1666, is the two-room deep plan with side circulation. Another variation placed a chimney in the center of the two-room deep plan. In Philadelphia, Boston, and other mid-Atlantic region cities, the latter plan was used with some frequency, although modified to place the stair between the chimney and the partition between the rooms. A variation favored in New England was similar to London examples in possessing front and rear rooms on each story with the stair between them. An inte-

rior passage from the front of the house to the stair exists in most of the known examples of this type in America. Other houses with two rooms per floor used outside passages in lieu of an internal hallway to access the stair at the center of the plan. As Herman points out, the alternative plans accommodated many possible uses of the small spaces, for both work and residence.[8]

The order and uniformity that British architects, government agents, and speculators sought to establish in the residential areas of London, Bath, and other cities from the second half of the seventeenth century were conspicuously absent in many early-American settlements. Boston, for example, became notorious for its lack of a coherent urban plan and for its tortuously winding street pattern. As the architecture critic Russell Sturgis wrote in *Scribner's Magazine* in June 1890, recalling old Boston, "The New Yorker walking along the Boston streets had a curious sensation of brushing the walls of the houses with his elbow, and of being within two feet of the people looking out of the windows of the ground floor....the narrow and crooked streets, lined on both sides with houses like these, gave a singular air of sternness and simplicity to the town, and caused to a certain extent what was called the English look of Boston." Clearly, Sturgis was thinking *not* of eighteenth-century efforts to regularize English houses and cities, but instead of the traditional English town, in which diverse houses were jumbled together along the major streets. In Bernard Herman's more recent reconstruction, the diverse appearance of houses around Garden Court Street and North Square, in Boston's North End neighborhood (near the Paul Revere House), likewise results in a picture of urban density. He emphasizes the variety of house types — some drawn from English examples — that coexisted in the North End through the late-eighteenth century and that "shaped a particular cityscape defined by qualities of juxtaposition." Such variety in Boston houses, and indeed in the domestic architecture of other cities, was romanticized in the nineteenth century when the quirky irregularity of traditional settlements was eradicated by later progress. But even before industrialization and rapid urbanization imposed greater regularity on housing in the second half of the nineteenth century, a preference for uniformity arose with the arrival of the new American republic.

Paul Revere House, Boston, ca. 1681, as restored. Rear elevation photographed in July of 1979.

Paul Revere House. Front elevation in 1941.

Paul Revere House hall (south room, first floor).

The Townhouse in the Early Republic

The townhouse type was politicized in a way that made it consistent with post-revolutionary Republicanism, and that meaning turned precisely on the sameness of the buildings. The similarity between the elements in the row was thought to correspond to the equality guaranteed by the Republic. This Republican egalitarian claim drew attention away from the real limitations to equality that existed, based on race, gender, and social and economic status. As historian Gwendolyn Wright points out, the sameness of houses implied the ability of all Americans to own one, at the very moment, after the Revolution, that property was becoming more expensive in cities like New York: "As the architectural imagery of egalitarianism took form," she writes, "the actual economic conditions in American cities became more stratified."[9] The point of the "fabrick of Freedom," as it was called in the period, was to rein in expressions of individual achievement while maintaining an overall sameness expressive of community interests. Even before the Revolution, American townhouses in Philadelphia,

Annapolis, Maryland, and elsewhere, under the influence of the English Georgian models, had a greater degree of uniformity. In Philadelphia and Charleston, urban regularity had been further enhanced by early grid plans. The original plan of the former city had even anticipated four open squares in the residential quarters of the city. Around the time of the Revolution, however, stylistic consistency took on political implications and coincided with the popularization — by architects and published builders' guides — of the British Palladian style.

The rise of interest in architectural regularity took place at the same moment as the first emergence of architecture as a profession in the United States. Although "gentlemen" practitioners (like Thomas Jefferson) were the rule through the middle of the nineteenth century when the first American architecture schools were founded, in the Early Republic many professional designers in the former colonies turned to townhouse design. In Baltimore, New York, Boston, and Portland, Maine, these architects helped counteract what Jefferson and other

Small-scale Federal-style rowhouses in Annapolis, Maryland.

A 1936 photograph showing small-scale early nineteenth-century rowhouses in Baltimore.

critics saw as the aesthetically meager character of American cities and their architecture. The first professionals contributed by designing rows of residences that drew on the models of contemporary European and British architecture, and by using those houses to frame residential squares. Such projects became the mechanisms for expanding the growing cities of the East Coast.

Among the earliest professional architects to practice in the United States was Benjamin Henry Latrobe (1764–1820) who was born in England and trained in Germany and England, although his work also demonstrated a familiarity with eighteenth-century French architecture. To great public projects like the United States Capitol, the Baltimore Cathedral, and the State Penitentiary in Richmond, Virginia, Latrobe brought his sophisticated drawing abilities and knowledge of British and Continental neoclassicism. He also contributed to townhouse design. In Philadelphia, Thomas Carstairs (1749–1830), who has also been credited with popularizing British neoclassicism in the United States, and Latrobe built two back-to-back rows on Sansom and Walnut

streets between 1800 and 1803. Aesthetically, the two rows perpetuated features of Anglo-American rowhouses of the second half of the eighteenth century: The red brick facades are tied together by white stone belt courses and the doorways are surmounted by small fanlights.

Groups of rowhouses in the Palladian mode were designed in Philadelphia and Baltimore by Robert Mills (1781–1855), who had studied with Latrobe. Mills is credited with the designs of Franklin Row in Philadelphia (1809) and Waterloo Row in Baltimore (1816–1819). In both of these projects, the design of the row as a unified composition drew on the example of Robert Adam and other British terrace designers. In further response to the British Palladianism, Mills used fanlights and sidelights around the doors and three-part ("Palladian") windows with arches above on the facades.[10] Among the other American architects who learned from Latrobe, and who contributed to the development of the rowhouse type, was William Small, who designed a row of eight three-and-one-half story dwellings in 1819, in the Seton Hill neighborhood of Baltimore, for

Waterloo Row, Baltimore, 1816–1819,
photographed in 1936. Robert Mills, Architect.

Waterloo Row, Baltimore, 1816–1819. Robert
Mills, Architect. Nineteenth-century photograph.

Pascault Row, Baltimore, 1819. Attributed to William Small, Architect. Photographed in 1936.

House in Charleston, South Carolina, ca. 1800, with later alterations and additions.

Single House, Charleston, South Carolina, ca. 1840.

the wealthy French-born merchant Louis Pascault. Pascault Row, as it was known, has been called the "last remaining example of early 19th-century town-houses" (by the National Park Service) in Baltimore. With their taut and almost unornamented brick facades, the houses embody the prevalent Federal style of the period 1780–1820, which was inspired by English Georgian and Palladian architecture.

Smaller versions of Pascault Row, sometimes even lacking a side hall, were constructed in Baltimore for middle- and working-class people. However, a 1799 ordinance required brick construction to prevent fire. In Charleston, where a special version of the townhouse evolved during the Federal period, both masonry and wood frame continued to be used. The "Charleston single" house-type that defines large areas of the city was distinctive for having a three-bay multistory facade placed close to the street, with a one-story side projection containing an entrance to a piazza along the side of the building. At the center of the side wall was an entrance to the main hallway. The piazza's second story usually offered a view over a side garden and of the city beyond, and was oriented to take advantage of pre-

vailing breezes as a defense against Charleston's hot climate. The distinctive arrangement of the Charleston single, with its narrow gable end toward the street, is believed to have grown out of earlier buildings that combined residential and commercial spaces. With its side yard and service areas extending to the rear of the lot, the Charleston single also responded to the model of the low-country plantation, in which formal living spaces and service functions had been architecturally separate.[11]

British Palladianism, Continental stylistic influences, and predominant forms of English urbanism all informed the work of Boston's influential "gentleman architect" Charles Bulfinch. Although Bulfinch had been liberally, rather than professionally, educated at Harvard, he subsequently traveled and studied in London, eventually becoming a professional. He was also deeply involved with municipal matters and, as a real estate speculator, closely associated with Boston's expansion. Bulfinch's Tontine Crescent project (1794), a group of speculatively-built townhouses, underscored his reliance on British architecture and urbanism, and demonstrated how unified streetscapes could be used to frame a residential square, thereby giving the city a more formal and imposing character and enlarging it in the process. As Ashton R. Willard commented in *The New England Magazine* in 1890 with respect to the Tontine Crescent: "Not all the curves in old Boston streets were made by cows in their uncertain wanderings. One at least was carefully designed and represents an importation into this country at a very early day of the ambitious plan of giving an aesthetic character to city streets, which was finding favor in London toward the close of the last century." Bulfinch was widely credited, during and after his lifetime, for having brought the neoclassical idiom, popularized in England by the Adams, to Boston. The flat, regularized facades of the Tontine Crescent with their neoclassical details stemmed from such projects as the Adams' Adelphi Terrace. His design treatment of the whole crescent as one composition with a focal

point at the center was likely also inspired by the Adams. At the Tontine Crescent the center pavilion contained a passage through the building at the first story; the upper story was detailed with paired columns framing a Palladian window. Bulfinch also borrowed the urban concept of stringing all the houses along a gracefully curved line to frame a central green space from British precedents in London and Bath. As Willard reports, the "semi-oval park space which the old deeds provided should be forever left open 'for the accommodation convenience and beauty' of the houses in the square" had as its focal point a neoclassical urn.

Although Bulfinch was bankrupted by the Tontine Crescent project, he continued to play an active role in Boston's expansion. In 1808, in his capacity as a member of the Board of Selectmen, Bulfinch provided a plan for filling in a portion of

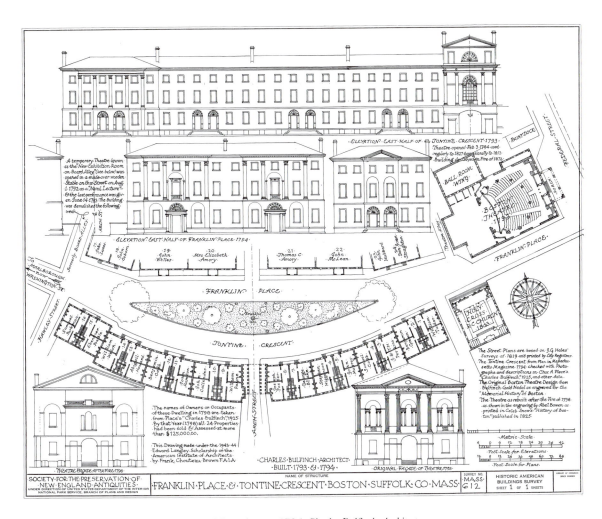

Franklin Place and Tontine Crescent, Boston, Massachusetts, 1794. Charles Bulfinch, Architect.

Louisburg Square, Boston, planned 1826.

the Mill Pond — the famous "Bulfinch triangle" — adjacent to the present North Station, to add to Boston's limited territory, the fill coming at least in part from the decapitation of Beacon Hill. As Nancy Seasholes has shown, filling tidal areas was a continual strategy employed to expand Boston's original restricted territory. Filled lands in the Back Bay, South End, and other neighborhoods provided large new tracts for the erection of townhouses through the nineteenth century.[12]

Both the concept of the residential square and the Palladian neoclassical style became part of the design vocabulary of non-professionals as a consequence of emulation and through a variety of publications aimed directly at carpenter-builders. The Tontine Crescent with its green Franklin Place before it, modeled on the English residential squares, inspired the Mount Vernon Proprietors to plan Louisburg Square on Beacon Hill in 1826, although

the houses were not built until 1833 to about 1847. The houses lining the lower side of the slightly sloping site possess bowed facades, a feature commonly associated with Boston rowhouses, and which had formerly been used by Bulfinch and others for larger town and country houses. Not only was the private residential square adopted by followers of Bulfinch, but so was his rowhouse style. For example, Asher Benjamin's elevations and plans for a townhouse in one of his many books were inspired by Bulfinch. The stark facade is nearly unornamented, save for a belt course above the English basement and contrasting stone lintels above the side entrance and windows. The plan Benjamin illustrates recalls seventeenth- and eighteenth-century types with its side circulation and two main rooms per floor. At the main or "parlor" level, however, the two rooms open onto one another through a wide doorway in the partition between them. The resulting "double-parlor" would remain a feature of townhouses through the nineteenth century. As the Greek Revival emerged in residential design at the middle of the century, the doorway would be marked — in the grander houses — by a pair of columns.

The Greek Revival Townhouse

Asher Benjamin and other authors, through their publications of designs loosely based on the buildings of antiquity, contributed to the emergence of the Greek Revival in the 1830s. The aesthetic preference for massive Greek forms was supported in part by American identification with Greece in that country's war for independence fought against the Ottoman Empire between 1821 and 1832. As an American chronicler of the conflict, Samuel G. Howe commented in 1828: "The revolution now in progress in Greece, differing certainly in some important respects from our own, is in others of equal importance." The Greek Revival style was so ubiquitous by the 1840s that some critics claimed that every manner of building sported columns and pediments to the extent

Greek Revival cornice and dormers of Tillary House, photographed in 1935.

that it was impossible to tell one type from another, a bank and a church having become virtually indistinguishable. Not only public and religious buildings, but residences also adopted the Greek-inflected style while still hewing to the urban functions they had come to perform during the Early Republic.

The basic rowhouse plan of the early national period was essentially preserved and cloaked in Greek details. The common arrangement of a side entrance hall with two major rooms on each floor persisted although, as Charles Lockwood pointed out, the proportions of the Greek Revival house were taller. The earlier arrangement that placed the kitchen and dining room below the stoop was maintained but those rooms gained higher ceilings. Double parlors on the first floors reached ceiling heights as great as fourteen feet while the upper levels of bedrooms were smaller in scale.[13] Enhancing the classical impression of the exteriors was the substitution of a full third story with a flat roof above for the earlier, Federal, arrangement in which two-story houses had been surmounted by steeply pitched gabled roofs punctuated with dormers. Athenaeum Row, a group of Greek Revival houses on Providence, Rhode Island's College Hill, designed by architect Russell Warren in 1845, are three full stories tall with a half-story lit by eyebrow windows above. The roof is extremely shallow and nearly invisible from the street.

The Greek Revival's popularity coincided with the rise in status of New York City to a "capital of the country" as Samuel F. B. Morse, the painter and

Greek Revival doorway of Dr. James Tillary House, Brooklyn, 1813–20, photographed in 1935, just before its demolition.

Seven (left) and 8 Washington Square North,
New York City, 1832–33, photographed in 1934.

Front parlor of 8 Washington Square North,
New York City, 1832–33, photographed in 1934.

Colonnade Row (La Grange Terrace), New York City, 1833, photographed in 1998. Seth Geer, Architect.

inventor, put it in 1831. Following the opening of the Erie Canal in 1825, which connected the city with the Midwest, New York exploded as a commercial, intellectual, and cultural center, its population soaring from 125,000 in 1825 to 815,000 by the Civil War. The city's northward expansion on the island of Manhattan was propelled, in part, by the speculative development of rows of Greek Revival townhouses. Greek Revival rows survive in several areas of lower Manhattan, including Washington Square North, St. Mark's Place, Greenwich Village, and Chelsea. In 1831 Samuel B. Ruggles planned Gramercy Park between Twentieth and Twenty-first Streets on Manhattan's east side. At the center of the development was a private park, one and a half acres in size, and surrounded by sixty lots. In the ensuing decades, Gramercy Park was lined with Greek Revival houses. With access to the private park at the center, these houses became some of the most desirable addresses

in New York City. Samuel J. Tilden, elected governor of New York in 1874, occupied the 1845 Greek Revival brownstone at Number 15 Gramercy Park South, which was later transformed in a renovation by the firm of Vaux & Radford, and which now serves as the headquarters of the National Arts Club. Gramercy Park represented the continuation of the British model of urban organization. Over time, the general tendency in urban design was to have park space be at least nominally public. However, Gramercy Park, like Louisburg Square, remains private.

The rows of houses surrounding these nineteenth-century parks were consistent, even repetitive in some places, but they were not treated as single compositions. In New York City, one group of rowhouses that did represent a unified design was the Colonnade Row. Designed and built by Seth Geer, the houses were joined by a two-story marble colonnade above a rusticated first story. The prestige of

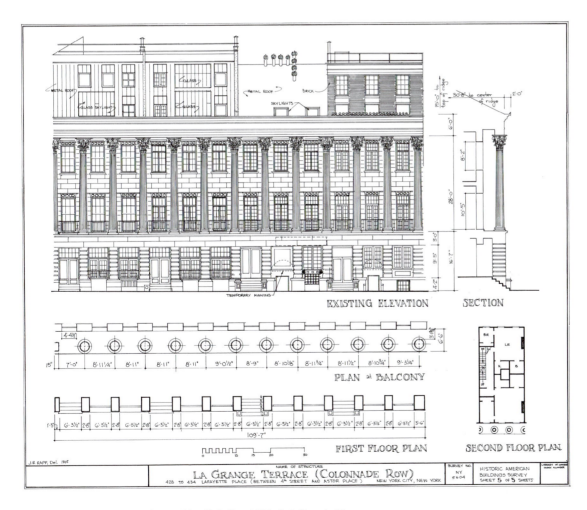

Colonnade Row (La Grange Terrace), New York City, 1833. Seth Geer, Architect.

Linden Row, Richmond, Virginia, 1847–53. Otis Manson, Architect. Two houses in the row were demolished in 1922 and the remainder purchased by Richmond preservationist Mary Wingfield Scott.

the residences derived from their expensive materials, up-to-date style, and the monumentality that resulted from treating the adjoining facades comprehensively. While projects like the Colonnade Row met the housing needs of the wealthy, as architectural historian Dell Upton has shown, the type of the rowhouse was also adapted during the middle decades of the nineteenth century to respond to the growth in New York's middle- and working-class populations. Smaller-scale rowhouses, as well as adjoining houses divided into tenements, filled in some of the grid's blocks as the city expanded northward.[14] The hierarchy of rowhouses resulted from differences in scale, as well as materials. While the most prestigious Greek Revival houses were in stone and brick, other examples approximated the columns and entablatures in wood and iron. In Manhattan, as well as in Brooklyn and Staten Island, attached wood-frame houses with Greek Revival details show the prevalence of mid-century wooden rowhouses that accommodated those who could not afford the very grandest and most stylish residences. Mid-century interest in Greek architecture extended across the country but melded with local traditions to produce regional variations of the Greek Revival style, partic-

ularly with respect to rowhouses. For example, in New Orleans, following the fire of 1794, three-story townhouses began to replace the one-story residences that had been common. Given the strong French influence in New Orleans culture, it is not surprising that the particular form of townhouse that gained currency there was inspired by Parisian examples. It was common in New Orleans to have one main block at the street (the *corps de logis*) with a courtyard behind it and a second service block (the *garçonnière*) at the rear of the property.

Among the architects who dominated the profession in New Orleans during the mid-nineteenth century was the Irish-born James Gallier, Sr. (1798–1866), who had formed a partnership with the neoclassical architect Minard Lafever (1797–1854) in New York before traveling to the South in the mid-1830s. Gallier brought to New Orleans a deep appreciation for Classical architecture, a sentiment he had revealed in an earlier lecture in Brooklyn in which he stated that "The character of the genuine architecture of the Greeks, in their brightest days…is that of an imposing grandeur united to pleasing simplicity, elegance of ornament, and harmony of proportion in an eminent degree." Two of Gallier's residential commissions in New Orleans were for Micaela Almonester, Baroness de Pontalba, the daughter of a wealthy New Orleans family, who had lived most of her life in France. Driven back to New Orleans by the Revolution of 1848, she resolved to build two identical residential properties on the Place d'Armes in the Vieux Carré, possibly inspired by the Place des Vosges in Paris. Quarreling with Gallier, de Pontalba brought in architect Henry Howard (1818–1884) to complete the plans for the buildings, which were finished in 1850 and 1851. Each of the buildings contains sixteen three-story houses and together frame the Place d'Armes, renamed Jackson Square in 1851.[15] The buildings possess some classical details as well cast-iron railings around the porches on their facades, a characteristic feature of New Orleans architecture. More importantly, the residences function in the way that the houses around earlier Parisian squares did, to contain and monumentalize an important public space.

In Boston, Greek Revival elements were accommodated within the preexisting townhouse type. For example, Alexander Parris (1780–1852) designed

the David Sears House (ca. 1819) on Beacon Street, facing Boston Common, with a familiar bow-front facade but with a columned porch in the Greek manner. Constructed of granite, a material favored for commercial building in Boston, in 1832 the once freestanding house was doubled in size and joined to the house of Harrison Gray Otis. As the city of Boston grew through the 1820s and 1830s, the continued filling of tidal areas provided additional space for the development of rowhouses that incorporated Greek Revival elements. For instance, in 1828, along Beacon Street, opposite the Public Garden, the Mount Vernon Proprietors erected a group of rowhouses on filled land. While these houses retained the three-bay facades of Federal-period houses, they were constructed of granite, and the more refined detailing of the earlier buildings gave way to a simplified treatment that emphasized the massiveness of the stone facades.

The epitome of the Greek Revival in domestic architecture was undoubtedly the temple-front house. That type was, however, better adapted to a house that stood on a large lot than to a rowhouse or townhouse. Nonetheless, in several towns and cities the

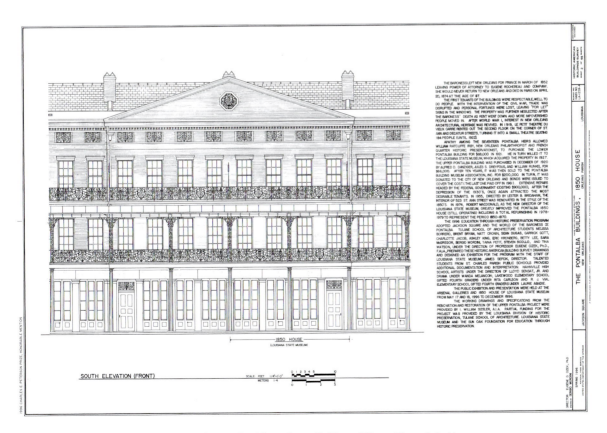

Pontalba Buildings, Jackson Square, New Orleans, Louisiana. James Gallier and Henry Howard, Architects.

West Brick, Middle Brick, and East Brick, Nantucket Island, Massachusetts, 1838.

Greek Revival was adjusted to suit townhouse construction and the definition of public spaces. For example, on Nantucket Island, twenty miles off the shore of Massachusetts's Cape Cod, numerous Greek Revival houses were built along the village's Main Street and collectively established an impressive street facade. The best-known are the three houses — known as West Brick, Middle Brick, and East Brick — constructed by ship owner Joseph Starbuck in 1838 for his three sons. They are essentially Federal-period townhouses with Ionic porticos added, evidence of the increasing awareness among local builders of Greek architecture. Several years later, around the time of the major Nantucket fire of 1846, other houses were constructed with temple fronts. The ways in which Main Street's Greek Revival houses held a line relatively close to the street, and incorporated fashionable forms into existing domestic typologies, gave the thoroughfare an urban feeling

expressive of the island's prosperity. The first modern historian of the American Greek Revival, Talbot Hamlin, described Nantucket as "one of the most harmonious and attractive of American seaport towns. The effect of the town as one strolls through it is exactly as that intended by its builders of a century ago…there is a definite sense of composition, of harmony in design, a careful choice of materials…the living expression of community life as the people of the Greek Revival desired it to be."[16]

The bedrock of prosperity on which that community had been built collapsed when the whale hunt declined in the second half of the nineteenth century as alternative lighting fuels to whale oil were developed. It was only at the end of the century, with the rise of tourism, that Nantucket once again thrived and its village architecture was preserved. The fall and rise of Nantucket was paralleled by a decline and rehabilitation in critical esteem for Greek Revival

Mid- to late-nineteenth-century rowhouses in Baltimore. Photographed in 1936.

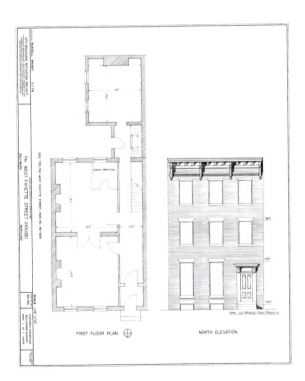

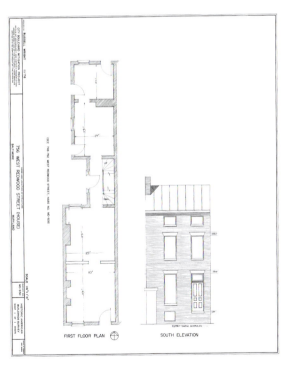

House, West Fayette Street, Baltimore, ca. 1860. The facade typifies the Italianate style with its pronounced cornice, while the plan follows those of earlier rowhouses.

House, West Redwood Street, Baltimore, ca. 1850. The small scale of the house precludes a side hall, and the entrance leads directly into the front parlor.

Van Vorst Park, Jersey City, New Jersey. Postcard view, 1905.

architecture. At the end of the nineteenth century critic Montgomery Schuyler described Greek Revival townhouses as "bald and dull" and, in 1927, historian Thomas Tallmadge wrote in *The Story of American Architecture* that "of all the exotic styles that have captured the American taste, the Greek Revival was the most exotic and of our provincialism the most flagrant example." Over the course of the next several decades, however, the Greek Revival would be rehabilitated, along with a host of other nineteenth-century styles, each of which had an impact on the American townhouse.

The Italianate Brownstone

Perhaps the rowhouse style that has endured the greatest fluctuations in popularity is the Italianate brownstone. Interest in Italian Renaissance and Baroque architecture, and in the ways that those historic modes could be adapted to urban residential building, coincided with the rapid expansion of cities throughout the United States in the decades surrounding the Civil War. The headlong growth of commercial and industrial centers through the 1850s and 1860s spurred the development of vast neighborhoods of rowhouses suited for both working-class people and middle-class families. The scales of the Italianate brownstones built for the middle class

were generally larger than middling houses of the earlier periods, although since typical street frontages did not expand (and indeed sometimes narrowed), the buildings were often simply made taller in order to increase their impressiveness. The results were high ceilings and elongated windows. Elements that were intended to relate to Italian precedents included boldly scaled window and door hoods and sometimes quoins at the corners of the facades. However, the most outstanding, and most often criticized, characteristic of these houses was their uniformity. As a consequence of the speculative construction of entire rows of houses, and as an outgrowth of a general preference among builders and owners for uniformity among the facades, house forms were seemingly endlessly repeated. The sameness that monumentalized a row of houses could also contribute to what some saw as a kind of deadening visual monotony over a number of urban blocks. It was the architectural analogue to what nineteenth-century social critics saw as the dreary depersonalization visited by the new city of the industrial age on its crowded, anonymous citizens. Novelist Edith Wharton described the homogenizing effect of the material when she wrote in *The Age of Innocence* about "the brownstone of which the uniform hue coated New York like a cold chocolate sauce." It was only in the mid-twentieth century that the "Brownstone Blitz" was described in more positive terms and rowhouse neighborhoods once again became highly desirable places of residence.

Brownstones redefined older American cities in two ways. First, rows of them dominated the streets of all of the larger cities that grew dramatically in the decades around the Civil War. Second, they were used by developers in the way that earlier rowhouses had been used, that is, to define the boundaries of parks and squares that served as oases in the densely built cities. For example, in Jersey City, New Jersey — just across the Hudson River from the west side of lower Manhattan — two residential squares were developed during the mid-nineteenth century, Van Vorst Park and Hamilton Park. The latter is believed to have been planned by John Coles in 1804 but development did not begin until the 1840s, and the brick and brownstone rowhouses that surround it are mostly of a later date. In Boston, the "New" South End, developed mostly between 1851 and 1859, on made land, contained several residential squares around long, narrow, and lozenge-shaped, block-long parks. These squares, as well as the other streets of the South End, were lined with brick and brownstone rowhouses in the Italianate style and recalled the earlier Louisburg Square as well as its British precedents. On many blocks, the houses perpetuated the bow-front form familiar from earlier Boston neighborhoods, although the proportions of the South End buildings were far taller than those of their predecessors. Scale was one factor that distinguished the South End Italianate-style residences from the city's earlier rowhouses. Another, according to one of the neighborhood's first historians, Bainbridge Bunting, was the monotonous repetition of "the same unit of design" which, together with the curving facades, gave the South End "a droning plasticity."[17]

Nearly identical Italianate facades constructed of brick and brownstone also lined South Park, the residential square laid out in San Francisco by the British-born speculator "Lord" George Gordon in 1854. Although the framing blocks of mirror-image, three-bay rowhouses have been lost, the lozenge-

Aerial view of South Park, San Francisco, showing the planning of a neighborhood of townhouses.

top: *Rowhouses with Italianate details in Old Town Alexandria, Virginia.*

bottom: *Rowhouses on Capitol Hill, Washington, D.C., showing the varieties of houses that accommodated an economically diverse population during the middle decades of the nineteenth century.*

shaped park remains. South Park and adjacent Rincon Hill were quite fashionable in the mid-nineteenth century, but the development of Nob Hill, after the introduction of the cable car in 1873, made the steeper slopes of the latter more appealing. One of the significant dynamics demonstrated by the histories of the South End and South Park — as well as those of other brownstone areas — is the degree to which rowhouse neighborhoods were subject to rapid rises and declines in popularity and social prestige, with significant implications for the preservation of the buildings themselves.

The fall from favor of the brownstone rowhouse quickly obliterated memories of its first appeal. Although critics of the brownstone denounced what they saw as the boring repetition of its form, the stone front had originally been introduced in order to counteract what was seen as the overuse of the Greek Revival style in rowhouse construction. For instance, the English author Frances Trollope wrote in *Domestic Manners of the Americans* (1832) that, "The great defect in the houses is their extreme uniformity — when you have seen one, you have seen all." In this context, as Herbert Croly commented in *The Architectural Record* in 1903, "[T]he brownstone which has since become the peculiar symbol of architectural monotony was welcomed as affording an agreeable variety to the insipid repetitions of New York dwelling houses." In Manhattan, brownstone was used extensively in neighborhoods above twenty-third street that were developed around the middle of the nineteenth century. Croly considered the construction of the Vanderbilt houses on Fifth Avenue during the early 1880s as the height of the brownstone fad, after which "it was abandoned so rapidly, both by speculative builders and by the richer men who built their own houses, that the sudden change can only be accounted for on the ground, partly, no doubt, unconscious, of an utter weariness of the flesh and spirit."

During the few decades in which the brownstone dominated residential construction in Manhattan, Brooklyn, and other cities, it offered a number of qualities that made the type appeal to contemporary tastes. First, the rich colors in which brownstone was available were consistent with the predominant palettes of textiles, furnishings, wallpaper, and paint during the middle decades of the nineteenth century. Second, sandstone is relatively soft and easily worked into wide door hoods, window lintels, brackets, and other details. Third, the depth of detailing made possible by the use of brownstone created vivid shadows and contrasts of light and dark areas on the facades of houses. This effect was very different from that of the flat Federal-style or Greek Revival rowhouse facade from earlier in the century. Furthermore, the changing visual display that resulted on brownstone facades corresponded to a favorable attitude toward subjective and changeable experiences of architecture that arose from the mid-century Romantic movement.

Although brownstone can therefore be understood as having produced the kinds of visual sensations that corresponded with the aesthetic ideals of the mid-nineteenth century, and as having made possible lavish displays that the growing bourgeois class desired to make, the material did offer some drawbacks. These are still being addressed by brownstone owners today. As *Putnam's Monthly Magazine* commented in 1853, when cut and laid correctly, brownstone was a reliable material. A sedimentary rock, sandstone or freestone naturally occurs in layers, and "is very soft and friable, *in the direction of its grain*, but sufficiently tough and durable in the other direction; so that, when laid in the wrong way, not only is it more exposed to the corroding influences of the atmosphere, allowing the dampness of our rains and snows more easily to penetrate its exposed pores, but it is liable to crack and fall off in scales." The recommendation to lay brownstone with its layers parallel to the ground plane, rather than parallel to the wall plane, in which position they tended to flake off, was not universally attended to. The result was the exfoliation of the brownstone fronts of many rowhouses. Another factor in the durability of brownstone was the quality of the material itself, which varied along with its color. New York City's brownstone was quarried in a number of relatively nearby locations, including Little Falls, New Jersey, on the Passaic River and in the vicinity of Portland, Connecticut.

Several Brooklyn neighborhoods were transformed by a building boom during the second half of the nineteenth century into what are arguably the nation's foremost collections of brownstones. From Brooklyn Heights, which looks across the East River to Manhattan and had been built up earlier in the century, residential development extended east to "The Hill," encompassing areas now known as Fort Greene and Clinton Hill. Fort Greene Park, known originally as Washington Park, was established in 1848 and completed by Frederick Law Olmsted and Calvert Vaux (Central Park's designers) two years later. To the east side of the park, on the street called Washington Park, several blocks of brownstone rowhouses were built between 1866 and 1867 with characteristically high stoops, wide window and door hoods, and substantial brackets supporting the roof cornice. These houses also had steeply-pitched Mansard roofs covered with slate tiles and sporting dormers, inspired by contemporary French Second-Empire architecture. The nearby Brooklyn Navy Yard, commissioned as early as 1801, provided employment for the neighborhood's diverse population, which included by the 1840s British and European immigrants as well as half of Brooklyn's African-American population.

In the 1870s, Prospect Park was completed to the design of Olmsted & Vaux, and the development of rowhouses followed in the area adjacent to the west side of the Park, now known as Park Slope. Construction of brownstones began in the late 1860s, when the area was recognized for its residential potential, but was cut short by the financial Panic of 1873.[18] *The Brooklyn Eagle* commented in 1884 on the construction of a "handsome row of brownstone houses" on Seventh Avenue in the north part of Park Slope, adding that, "So great is the demand for property in the neighborhood, that most of these are already engaged." While these North Slope brownstones were relatively expensive, the South Slope and adjacent Windsor Terrace dwellings were "intended for clerks and business people with small incomes," according to *The Brooklyn Eagle*. The houses, which rented for between $18 and $40 per month were, according to the newspaper, "constructed of cheap but good materials, and afford[ed] comfortable homes to their occupants." Thus variously sized rowhouses accommodated an economically diverse population.

In Brooklyn, the presence of parks and street trees alleviated what was considered (by *The Brooklyn Eagle*) to be "the horrible monotony of the brownstone fronts with their endless processions of steps canted against the house at the same angle and carried to the same height." The criticism that brownstones

that had been considered earlier as antidotes to the monotony of the Greek Revival rows had become boringly ubiquitous was voiced during and after the 1880s. Of the brownstone front, Montgomery Schuyler asked in *The Architectural Record* of 1899, "Who was the malefactor who first discovered the practicability of that scandalous edifice?" Schuyler objected to the overuse of the material which he criticized for having been intended to look "more costly and the house more valuable than in fact it was." Monotony and pretentiousness were not the only criticisms raised of the brownstone. For Schuyler and others, the convention of arranging the houses with a high stoop leading to a small vestibule and stairhall beyond allowed for little privacy from visitors, while its increased depth "made of the middle third of the house, a gloomy cavern." Fortunately, some of these aesthetic and functional defects would be addressed with the Queen Anne rowhouse during the last quarter of the nineteenth century.

The Queen Anne Townhouse

For cities that had existing townhouse traditions, the emergence of the Queen Anne style, adapted from the work of British designers like Richard Norman Shaw, transformed urban residential building. In cities that were starting to build large neighborhoods of attached or detached but closely-spaced houses, like Chicago following its great fire of 1871, the Queen Anne became the dominant stylistic mode. The Capitol Hill neighborhood of Washington, D.C., includes numerous Queen-Anne rows because its development began while Alexander "Boss" Shepherd — a speculator in residential construction in the neighborhood — was governor of the District between 1871 and 1874. The "Fan" neighborhood of Richmond, Virginia — named for the general outline of the streets that define it — was developed west of the city's commercial center between the 1880s and 1920s with Monument Avenue punctuated by sculptural figures of Confederate "heroes" at its center. The surrounding construction was of attached houses that exhibited features associated with the Queen Anne style, like towers, dormers, and varieties of windows and porches. In Philadelphia, which saw houses constructed at a rate of about 10,000 per year during the last two decades of the nineteenth century, the Queen Anne was the style of choice for wealthy homeowners on fashionable Walnut Street. As historian Jeffrey Alan Cohen suggests, the Queen Anne also played an important role in the construction of houses in fringe areas of downtown Philadelphia, where it encouraged architects to combine forms from various historic periods and to create visual diversity in the streetscapes.[19] In Brooklyn, the growth in popularity of the Queen Anne style brought about a distinct change in the appearance of new houses in comparison to those that had been built in the 1850s and 1860s. As *The Brooklyn Eagle* commented of the new Queen-Anne mansion of Mrs. F. S. Davenport in June, 1884, "The exterior is a composite of doors, windows, gables, and projections, and presents a strong contrast to the stately brown stone dwellings of the neighborhood."

While late nineteenth-century houses in New York, Washington, Richmond, and Philadelphia were largely brick — brownstone having been less readily available in those areas and out of fashion — the prevalent Queen Anne architecture of San Francisco was of wood frame because it was believed to be a more earthquake resistant material. The exterior sheathing and detailing associated with the Queen Anne — wood shingles and delicately turned elements — lent themselves to materials available in California. Inside these Queen Anne houses, according to architect John Wellborn Root writing in *Homes in City and Country* (1893), reigned "marvelous wallpaper, portieres, *bric-à-brac*, and Eastlake furniture," while stained glass enjoyed "a most shameless career."

The rise of the Queen Anne style's popularity coincided with the development in the United States of institutions that promoted professional architectural practice. These included schools of architecture, professional associations, and journals aimed at practitioners. Architects in established urban centers used all of these forums to debate the Queen Anne style. The very name "Queen Anne" was a misnomer since adherents of the style did not limit themselves to reviving just architectural forms that dated to the early eighteenth-century reign of Queen Anne. Instead, following in the footsteps of Richard Norman Shaw and other British architects, they incorporated elements drawn from the entire gamut of pre-modern architecture, ranging from medievalisms, like half-timbering and leaded glass windows, to classical features such as scrolled cornices over doors and windows

Facade and detail views of Queen Anne-style townhouses in San Francisco.

House by J. Appleton Wilson at North Calvert Street, Baltimore, published in the American Architect and Building News *(1879).*

Cartoon by Mary Petty, "In the brownstone facades the gaping spaces were soon filled." T. H. Robsjohn-Gibbings, Goodbye, Mr. Chippendale *(1944).*

and pedimented dormers. Boston architect Robert Peabody (1845–1917) lectured the Boston Society of Architects and wrote in the newly founded *American Architect and Building News* in 1877 concerning the Queen Anne, then ongoing in England. As Peabody suggested, whereas British architects had revived their earlier architecture, Americans might do the same with the vernacular buildings of the seventeenth and eighteenth centuries. He wrote, "To those who do believe in revivals, 'Queen Anne' is a very fit importation into our offices. There is no revival so little of an affectation on our soil, as that of the beautiful work of the Colonial days. Its quiet dignity and quaintness and elegance, always attract us. It is our legitimate field for imitation, and we have much of it to study right in our own neighborhood." Peabody undoubtedly contributed to the use of the Queen Anne style in urban houses in the developing area of Boston's Back Bay and in growing neighborhoods of other cities. In the following years the

American Architect and Building News would publish drawings of Queen Anne townhouses and rowhouses, among them the house at 1000 North Calvert Street in Baltimore, designed in 1877 by J. Appleton Wilson.

Wilson's townhouse and rowhouse designs showed the blend of historic details and the prevalent use of brick that are associated with the Queen Anne. Further, the plan of the Calvert Street house showed how fundamentally the Queen Anne had transformed the interiors of city residences. Already, at mid-century, critics had complained about the way that the sidehall plan created a dark space at the center of the rowhouse and had cited the manifest drawbacks of having visitors enter the house through a small vestibule and cramped stairhall. The obvious solution, encouraged by the planning flexibility that came with the Queen Anne, was to move the stairhall to the middle of the interior. Often lit from above by a skylight, the stairway could then be larger in size and take on some of the aspects of the "living hall" that had been popularized by Norman Shaw for suburban and country houses. Norman Shaw had demonstrated — and American architects had followed his lead — how the hall could be transformed into a cozy sitting area through the introduction of an overscaled hearth, stained glass window, ceiling beams, and other features. The drawback of adapting the living hall to the townhouse, according to Russell Sturgis, was that it ate up an enormous amount of space relative to its usefulness, especially in a city like New York where land was at a premium. For example, as architectural historian Sarah Landau has observed, in three rows of houses designed in 1883 to 1887 by Detlef Lienau on Eighty-second and Eighty-third Streets on Manhattan's Upper West Side, the central halls dwarfed the other spaces of the main living floor. At the centers of the blocks the houses were less than seventeen feet wide, making them relatively small in size, but the stairhalls at their centers were larger than the parlors.[20]

The Queen Anne movement, with its emphasis on the "picturesque" appearances of buildings contributed to the repudiation of consistency as an aspect of rowhouse and townhouse design. Regularity came to be considered less important as a variety of historicist styles came to the fore during the last quarter of the nineteenth century. Wealthy house builders were not limited to the Queen Anne, but could also select a French Renaissance or other exotic design. In 1944, illustrator Mary Petty caricatured this diversity when she drew a New York street where a "gap" in the brownstone facades had been filled with an ostentatious approximation of a French château.

The Colonial Revival and Neoclassical Townhouse
Robert Peabody argued in 1877 that the contemporary revival of earlier architecture in Britain — the Queen Anne movement — should inspire a parallel renewal of interest in American building from the pre-modern period. Peabody's rallying cry for the Colonial Revival was well-timed for it came just a year after the celebration of the Centennial of American independence, the cornerstone of which was the celebration held in Philadelphia's Fairmount Park. Like the Italianate brownstone before it, the Queen Anne rowhouse had its critics who believed that the proliferation of diverse forms it had brought about detracted from the visual harmony of the street. By

the turn of the century, tastes had turned away from exuberant details and rich colors, and a revival of interest in the plainer early American townhouse was born. Some of the Colonial Revival houses took as their visual points of departure the classic architecture of early American architects — like Charles Bulfinch and Benjamin Henry Latrobe — who had contributed to the development of the townhouse in the new United States. Thus some of the Colonial Revival rowhouses employed red brick with white stone and wood trim in the eighteenth-century manner. Elsewhere, limestone and other lighter colored materials were used. Often the details of these houses looked back to classical precedents and included carved and molded pilasters, friezes, cornices, and other motifs. And just as brownstone had complemented the colors used for interior décor at the century's mid-point, so limestone corresponded to the new palette then being promoted. In *The Decoration of Houses* (1897) by novelist Edith Wharton and architect-decorator Ogden Codman, Jr., the authors railed against the overwallpapered and draped interiors of the mid-nineteenth century. As an antidote to the overstuffed Victorian house, Wharton and Codman advocated white paint, light-colored fabrics, and French furniture.

The restraint Wharton and Codman advocated for interior design was paralleled by a call for greater consistency and harmony of streetscapes in the wake of the Queen Anne. The visual cacophony that had resulted from the adoption of late-nineteenth-century revival styles made the monotony of the Italianate brownstone look good. As Russell Sturgis wrote in 1893, "One advantage the brown-stone front had, and that was its conformity, its virtual uniformity. True, it was this repetition which made and makes a mile or so of it so dismal. But to a single block it gives a unity and keeping which its predecessor attained by more rational and artistic means, but which its successors have not attained at all." Sturgis blamed the contrast of neighboring houses on architects who wanted to advertise their design approaches, while others blamed the lack of taste of speculative builders.

New rowhouse neighborhoods from around the turn of the century adopted the neoclassical or Colonial Revival rowhouse as a dominant idiom while more established residential areas were filled in with buildings in the new styles. For instance, in the

George A. Nickerson House, Boston, 1895–97.
McKim, Mead and White, Architects.

Nickerson House, stair hall.

Striver's rowhouses, New York City, 1891. Bruce Price and Clarence S. Luce, Architects.

Prospect-Lefferts Gardens area of Brooklyn, adjacent to Prospect Park, more than 500 houses were built between 1905 and 1911. Most of these were constructed of white limestone and some echoed Federal-period rowhouses with flat and bowed facades and restrained details. Around 1890, in Harlem, a group of Colonial Revival houses was built on West 138th and 139th Streets, between Seventh and Eighth Avenues, to the design of Bruce Price and Clarence Luce, James Brown Lord, and McKim, Mead, and White. The prominent New York architecture firm had been in the forefront of the adaptation of classicism to public buildings, and, from the 1870s, its members had been active in recording early American architecture and using Colonial forms in domestic buildings. McKim, Mead and White's "King Model Houses" in Harlem, were part of an architecturally ambitious neighborhood known as "Striver's Row."

In Boston, the Back Bay was extended westward through filling operations that continued through the early twentieth century. West of Massachusetts Avenue, new streets like Bay State Road were lined with revivals of the city's Federal-period townhouses. Architect Arthur Little (1852–1925) built a house for himself at the corner of Bay State Road and Raleigh Street around 1890. Earlier, in 1878, he had published his drawings of Colonial and Federal-period houses as *Early New England Interiors*, and he pursued this interest in historic American architecture in his own house. Its shorter Bay State Road facade was bowed in imitation of Federal-period rowhouses and the longer Raleigh Street side incorporated Palladian windows, fanlights, and other details from the work of Bulfinch.

Little's house, like other Colonial Revival and neoclassical houses of the turn-of-the-century, represented more than an aesthetic repudiation of the mid-century brownstone: It also embodied a rethinking of traditional rowhouse planning. Along with the dark tones of the Italianate rowhouse, the prevalence of the high stoop had also been criticized. Arthur Little's house and others of the period replaced the high stoop with a short flight of steps. Often this entrance indicated the presence within not of a narrow sidehall — likewise the object of criticism — but instead of a commodious reception room. So influential was the new conception of the rowhouse entrance, that many earlier buildings had their steps

removed, their front entrances reworked, and the customary front basement dining room converted into a reception area.

The Modernist Townhouse

The Colonial Revival and neoclassical styles were arguably the last important stylistic developments in rowhouse design. After World War I, European modernist architecture exerted an important influence on American architecture, in both residential and commercial building. European modernist architects had been concerned with housing issues and many leaders of the movement had produced designs for attached houses. The Swiss-born architect William Lescaze (1896–1969), who immigrated to the United States in 1920, collaborated with his partner George Howe on the Philadelphia Savings Fund Society building (1930–32), a landmark of modernist design. Thereafter, he practiced in New York, building or renovating several rowhouses. Lescaze's own remodeled house at 211 East 48th Street in Manhattan adhered to the narrow street width of its urban lot, but broke from the nineteenth-century facades of its neighbors. Critic Lewis Mumford wrote in his *New Yorker* column (September 15, 1934) that, "Now Mr. Lescaze has pioneered the remodeling of a single unit, only seventeen feet in width, and shown what can be done within these drastic limits." The new front was distinguished by the use of glass block, curving white masonry, and a flat roof above the door, supported by a steel column and jutting into the space of the street.

Even as townhouse living declined in popularity for the upper class after World War II, some modernist architects continued to experiment with the housing type. The best example from the postwar period is the townhouse that architect Paul Rudolph (1918–1997) renovated and expanded for himself on Beekman Place in Manhattan in 1973. From the back of the existing building Rudolph projected a steel-frame extension and surmounted the house with a suspended terrace that capitalized on the view of the East River. On the interior, Rudolph's townhouse transgressed some of the salient features of the traditional residences that flanked it. Rudolph abandoned the conventional vertical arrangement of stories in the rowhouse by creating multiple levels within the building. Further, he used steel and glass to produce

William Lescaze House, New York City, 1934. William Lescaze, Architect. Front facade after renovation.

Lescaze House, rear elevation following renovation. William Lescaze, Architect.

open wells or views between the stories, thus piercing through the vertical divisions that ordinarily characterized attached urban houses. With its steel and glass roof structure, the Rudolph house seemed to climb up and over the staid Colonial Revival townhouses that surrounded it and that had made Beekman Place and Sutton Place quiet residential enclaves for the wealthy. As writer Louis Auchincloss commented, the fashionable part of Manhattan was traditionally the blocks between Central Park and Lexington Avenue, "but Mrs. William K. Vanderbilt and Miss Anne Morgan pushed it over as far as Sutton Place in the early 1920s," with the traditionalist townhouses they built there.

Despite the persistent appeal of certain neighborhoods in New York, as well as Beacon Hill and the Back Bay in Boston, Rittenhouse Square in Philadelphia, and Pacific Heights in San Francisco, townhouse living lost its appeal in the postwar period. The rapid physical and social collapse of many rowhouse neighborhoods in cities throughout the United States resulted from a growing absorption in the suburban ideal, bank lending policies that penalized socially diverse urban areas, and modernist planning that looked askance at the density and disorderliness of traditional neighborhoods. Even before World War II, fashion and land values initiated a move away from townhouses and toward apartment living. As Louis Auchincloss recalled of Manhattan's East Side: "In my childhood in the 1920s, the exodus from brownstones to apartments was already well under way; the building of a private house had become a rare sight. The increasing scarcity of servants and their dislike of having to run up and down stairs, plus the troubles of building maintenance, contributed to the abandonment of the old abodes, and by the 1950s, with more and more of the affluent choosing life in the suburbs, where schools were better and crime rarer, it began to look as if the East Side, always excepting the great apartment buildings on Fifth and Park Avenues, might degenerate into a shabby assemblage of tenements."

The busy disorderliness of tenement and rowhouse neighborhoods, anathema to modernist planners who preferred towering residences surrounded by open space, were championed in a 1961 book by Jane Jacobs, *The Death and Life of Great American Cities*. The book was a cry to resist the encroachment of modernist planning on traditional small-scale neighborhoods like Jacobs's own Greenwich Village in Manhattan. Although urban renewal projects continued to wipe out the older housing stock in many neighborhoods, the 1960s marked the beginning of a period of revitalization. Dissatisfaction with the sterility and homogeneity of suburban life, the inconvenience of living far from the workplace, and a renewal of interest in nineteenth-century architecture all contributed to the rediscovery of city living on the part of those who had the money to chose between the urban center and the suburban periphery. Savannah, for example, went from facing "a parking lot future" to renewed vitality. The method of saving the city was through historic preservation. The Historic Savannah Foundation, established in the 1950s, surveyed the city's older buildings, bought some and later sold them to owners who wanted to renovate. The Foundation's efforts focused on the townhouses from the eighteenth and nineteenth centuries, many of which framed the twenty residential squares that define Savannah as a city and that were redesigned and replanted at the same time. The renovation of a Greek Revival rowhouse by a formerly suburban family, profiled in *Southern Living* in 1972, typifies the architectural transformations that the rebirth of urban neighborhoods required. The floor level of the basement was lowered to create additional living space, brick walls were exposed, and smaller rooms on the upper floors combined to create an adequate kitchen.

Beginning in the 1960s the "Brownstone Revival" touched nearly all American cities. Indeed, the term "brownstoner" (a "preservationist or revivalist") — coined in the 1970s — illustrates how closely rowhouse renovation was associated with urban revitalization. As Deirdre Stanforth, the coauthor of *Buying and Renovating a House in the City* (1972), wrote, "The brownstone revival movement is catching all over America. In New York, in the nation's capital, in New England, the deep south and in the mid-west, people are discovering the beauty and utility of fine old houses and are restoring them." In the ensuing decades, townhouses in many American cities have been renovated as single-family homes or divided into smaller apartments. In those places where urban decay in the middle of the twentieth century led to the loss of blocks of houses or individual buildings,

Rowhouse, Savannah, ca. 1850, as renovated ca. 1970.

opportunities have arisen for creative infill construction. Since many rowhouse neighborhoods have been designated as local historic districts, this new construction often conforms to the scale and materials of the original buildings. Inventive solutions that combine modernist interiors and details with the massing of surrounding row houses exist in New York and other cities.

As middle- and upper-class homeowners have reclaimed derelict urban neighborhoods, tensions have risen with the poor who could never abandon the city centers. Escalating property values in newly popular rowhouse neighborhoods have driven out the poor, working-class, and minority groups who maintained their communities during the middle decades of the twentieth century, when wealthier inhabitants retreated to the suburbs. While such issues await resolution, the townhouse has taken on new appeal not only on aesthetic grounds but also on the basis of its social and environmental advantages. For the rowhouse neighborhood was above all a community in which the architectural form ensured a certain degree of sociability. The famous brownstone stoop provided a place to sit and commune with one's neighbors, to keep an eye on children at play, and to generally take part in city life. Such aspects of townhouse living could provide a solution to the urban problems we now face.

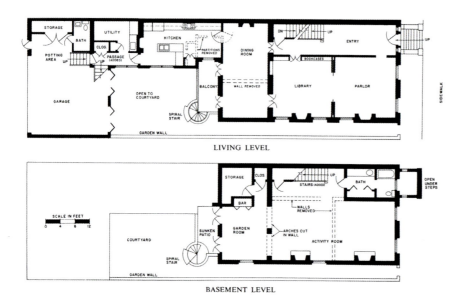

LIVING LEVEL

BASEMENT LEVEL

Plan of rowhouse, Savannah, ca. 1850, as renovated ca. 1970. Walls removed to create larger spaces and a more open plan are indicated with dashed lines.

Turn-of-the-century Philadelphia rowhouses with neoclassical features clad in aluminum, photographed in the 1970s.

Small-scale Philadelphia rowhouses from the second half of the nineteenth century, demonstrating the architectural uniformity some critics abhorred.

Early twentieth-century Philadelphia rowhouses with neoclassical porches and pedimented dormers.

Grove Street looking toward St. Luke's Chapel on Hudson Street, New York.

Numbers 16 (Players Club) and 15 (National Arts Club) Gramercy Park, New York.

Hudson and West Houston Streets, New York.

Bank Street near Ninth Avenue L train, New York.

Morris-Canby-Rumford Dollhouse, made by Caspar Wistar Morris in Philadelphia, ca. 1825, for his twin daughters, Elizabeth and Sarah. The dollhouse resembles the family's Market St. townhouse.

1. Ann Rooney Heuer, *Town Houses* (New York: Friedman/ Fairfax, 2000), 17.
2. Alexander Gorlin, *The New American Town House* (New York: Rizzoli, 1999), 10.
3. Emmanuel Le Roy Ladurie, *Montaillou* (New York: Random House, 1978), 3.
4. Fernand Braudel, "Pre-modern Towns" and W. G. Hoskins, "English Provincial Towns in the Early Sixteenth Century," both in Peter Clark, ed., *The Early Modern Town* (New York: Longman, 1976).
5. Hilary Ballon, *The Paris of Henri IV: Architecture and Urbanism* (Cambridge, MA: MIT Press, 1991).
6. Sir John Summerson, *Georgian London*, new ed. (London: Barrie Jenkins, 1988), 18–19.
7. Richard Sennett, *The Conscience of the Eye* (New York: Knopf, 1990), 93.
8. Bernard Herman, *Town House: Architecture and Material Life in the Early American City, 1780–1830* (Chapel Hill: University of North Carolina Press for the Ohmohundro Institute for Early American History and Culture, 2005).
9. Gwendolyn Wright, *Building the Dream: A Social History of Housing in America* (Cambridge, MA and London: MIT Press, 1983), 24–40.
10. Kenneth Ames, "Robert Mills and the Philadelphia Row House," *Journal of the Society of Architectural Historians* 27, no. 2 (1968): 140–6; William John Murtagh, "The Philadelphia Row House," *Journal of the Society of Architectural Historians* 16, no. 4 (1957): 8–13.
11. Martha A. Zierden and Bernard L. Herman, "Charleston Townhouses: Archaeology, Architecture, and the Urban Landscape, 1750–1850." In Rebecca Yamin and Karen Bescherer Metheny eds., *Landscape Archaeology: Reading and Interpreting the American Historical Landscape* (Knoxville: University of Tennessee Press, 1996), 204–7; Jessie Poesch, *The Art of the Old South: Painting, Sculpture, Architecture & the Products of Craftsmen* (New York: Knopf, 1983), 128–30.
12. Nancy Seasholes, *Gaining Ground: A History of Landmaking in Boston* (Cambridge, MA and London: MIT Press, 2003).
13. Charles Lockwood, *Bricks and Brownstone: the New York Row House, 1783–1929*, 2d ed. (New York: Rizzoli, 2003), 70.
14. Dell Upton, "Inventing the Metropolis: Civilization and Urbanity in Antebellum New York" in *Art and the Empire City: New York, 1825–1861*, Catherine Hoover Voorsanger and John K. Howat, eds. (New York: Metropolitan Museum of Art; New Haven: Yale University Press, 2000), 15–17.
15. William Nathaniel Banks, "The Galliers, New Orleans Architects," *The Magazine Antiques*, 151, no. 4 (April, 1997): 600–611.
16. Talbot Hamlin, *Greek Revival Architecture in America* (1944, Reprint. New York: Dover Publications, Inc., 1964), 171.
17. Bainbridge Bunting, *Houses of Boston's Back Bay: An Architectural History, 1840–1917* (Cambridge, MA and London: The Belknap Press of Harvard University Press, 1967), 69.
18. John B. Manbeck, ed., *The Neighborhoods of Brooklyn*, 2d ed. (New Haven: Yale University Press, 2004).
19. Jeffrey Alan Cohen, "The Queen Anne and the Late Victorian Townhouse in Philadelphia, 1878–1895," Ph.D. Diss., University of Pennsylvania, 1991.
20. Sarah Bradford Landau, "The Row Houses of New York's West Side," *Journal of the Society of Architectural Historians*, 34, no. 1 (Mar. 1975): 19–36.

Colonial and Federal

Mantua Maker's House

Philadelphia, Pennsylvania

Built in the middle of the eighteenth century, the house of Mary Smith and Sarah Milton represents the flexibility of the rowhouse type. Less than fifteen feet wide, the house's small scale, like the dimensions of neighboring houses, made it affordable for artisans who lived along Elfreth's Alley.

Elfreth's Alley began as a cart path in 1702, enabling the transportation of goods from the docks nearby on the Delaware River. In the middle of the eighteenth century, blacksmith Jeremiah Elfreth, a large landowner in the area, developed a number of rental properties along the alley to which he eventually lent his name. In 1762 Elfreth sold the house at number 126 Elfreth's Alley to two sisters-in-law, Mary Smith and Sarah Milton, who lived and worked together. Smith and Milton were mantua makers who produced cloaks and expensive garments. At the end of the eighteenth century, nearly a third of the households along Elfreth's Alley were headed by women, perhaps because the small-scale rowhouses were relatively affordable. The combination of residential and commercial uses that took place in the residence was typical of early Philadelphia houses in which the ground-floor front rooms were often used for shops. Historian Bernard Herman has found, through an inventory of the house's contents at the time of Smith's death in 1766, that the first-story room (the parlor) was intended to "inspire the confidence" of Mary Smith's and Sarah Milton's clients with "furnishings related to sociability and image": a tea table and tea wares, a dining table and dining wares, and a framed picture. The kitchen, located in an ell off the back of the house, contained pewter and earthenware vessels, as well as cooking equipment. The upstairs rooms, Herman suggested, lacked pretentious objects and were more private. The chamber over the kitchen may have been used for mantua-making. In 1794, at the time of her death, Milton was sharing the house with a younger mantua-maker named Elizabeth Carr. Milton's will granted Carr

tenancy in the house but stipulated that Carr's husband Alexander had no property rights nor any claim to Elizabeth's income.

In 1847 the house was sold to a German shoemaker named Lewis Kolb, who expanded the commercial use of the first-floor room by removing the staircase that had risen from it and cutting it off from the rest of the house. Kolb also purchased the adjoining house at number 124 Elfreth's Alley and built three-story tenements behind the two buildings. Kolb sold the Mary Smith and Sarah Milton House to a tenant, the German shoemaker John Schoendienst, in 1873. By that time there were twenty-seven people living at numbers 124 and 126 Elfreth's Alley and in the rear tenements, an indication of the crowding that existed in working-class American neighborhoods during the second half of the nineteenth century.[1]

In 1964 John B. Roberson explained to the readers of *Gentlemen's Quarterly* how, despite the boom in postwar suburban building, some of Philadelphia's vast rowhouse neighborhoods had been revitalized. Even small three-story houses with one room per floor — the "Father, Son, and Holy Ghost" houses — had been joined to adjacent buildings to create larger residences that met with modern requirements — "just big enough for a bachelor or a bride and groom." Elfreth's Alley was an important part of the rehabilitation of Center City Philadelphia. Although the houses were threatened with demolition in the 1940s, "the Elfreth's Alley Association fought doggedly just to keep colonial Philadelphia from being torn down by shortsighted commercial interests." Despite preservation efforts, urban renewal brought about the replacement of many historic neighborhoods with "ultra-modern town houses and apartment towers" in the Society Hill area and elsewhere. Restored by architect and historian Penny Batchelor, the Mantua Maker's House was opened as a museum by the Elfreth's Alley Association in the early 1960s and represents the eighteenth-century working-class neighborhood.

1. Elfreth's Alley Association, *Inside These Doors: A Guidebook of Elfreth's Alley Houses* (Philadelphia: Elfreth's Alley Association, 2003).

Entrance from Elfreth's Alley.

Stairway to the second story, which was at one point removed and subsequently restored.

opposite, top: The Mantua Maker's House as part of the row.

opposite, bottom: The narrowness of the street as well as the small scales of the adjoining houses. The Elfreth's Alley Association calls it "the oldest continuously inhabited street in America."

Main second-story room.

opposite, top: First-floor parlor.

*opposite, bottom: Kitchen with its hearth hung
with cooking utensils.*

Powel House

Philadelphia, Pennsylvania

The townhouse now known as the Powel House was built by a Scottish ship's master, Charles Stedman, in 1766. Five years earlier, the prosperous Stedman had purchased a lot on Third Street, near the Delaware River. The lot was twice as wide as normal residential lots in Philadelphia, measuring sixty feet at the street. Rather than build a "double" house, as was sometimes done, Stedman built a familiar side-entrance, three-bay rowhouse and used only half the width of the lot. The house possesses features typical of the mid-eighteenth century Georgian rowhouse in the Anglo-American tradition.

Almost before his house was completed, Charles Stedman had begun to suffer financial reversals. The house was advertised for sale as early as 1766 but not sold to the second owner, Samuel Powel, until 1769. At that time the house was not completed and Powel contracted with a carpenter-builder named Robert Smith (ca. 1722–1777) to finish the interior.[1] Powel was born in 1738 into a wealthy Quaker family and was educated at the College of Philadelphia. In 1769, two years following his return from Europe, Powel married Elizabeth Willing and purchased the Stedman house. Powel served as mayor both before and after the American Revolution. Powel was also a member of the Philadelphia Common Council for many years, an alderman, and a member of the Pennsylvania Senate. Elizabeth Powel played "the leading role in the family" and was described by the Marquis de Chastellux in his *Travels in North America in the Years 1780, 1781 and 1782*: "[S]he has not traveled, but she has wit and a good memory, speaks well and talks a great deal."

The Philadelphia known by the Powels was quite different than the one imagined by William Penn in 1681 when he instructed his commissioners: "Let every house be placed if the person pleases in the middle of its plat, as to the breath of it, that so there may be ground on each side for gardens or orchards or fields, that it may be a green town which will never be burnt and always be wholesome." The later plan of Philadelphia by surveyor Thomas Holme imagined a densely built city organized into squares with two main axes intersecting at the center of the grid. By the beginning of the nineteenth century, Philadelphia's population had tripled from its 1760 level as a result of shipping activity along the Delaware River.

The exterior of the Powel House reflected the preference for regularity that was a central feature of eighteenth-century townhouse and rowhouse design and it demonstrated the reliance of Philadelphia builders on English precedents. Like other contemporary houses in London and colonial cities, the house was constructed of brick with contrasting trim, which included granite belt courses dividing the stories of the facade and granite keystones in the window lintels. The door was framed by Doric columns which contrasted with the Ionic "frontispiece" on the adjoining Governor Byrd house, to the north, with which the Powel House was intended to harmonize visually. As was common in eighteenth-century Philadelphia, and in marked contrast to Penn's original notions, the house stood directly at the street and allowed no room for a garden.

The front block of the Powel House possessed an ample stair hall with two major rooms separated by a chimney on each floor. To the rear of the main block were "back buildings" or service areas, now connected to the front by a brick passage. The entrance and stair hall possesses some of the most impressive detailing in the building. As is the case in many grand Georgian houses, the passage is divided into two sections by an archway supported on pilasters. As the space that first greeted visitors to the house, it was appropriate that the hall be elaborately finished. Although many Philadelphia houses of the period had their best parlors on the ground floor, in this instance — and following British custom — the rooms on the second floor were more elaborately finished and likely served as reception areas for such well-known guests as George Washington and John Adams. It is likely that Powel was responsible for adding the

1. Charles E. Peterson et al., *Robert Smith: Architect, Builder, Patriot, 1722–1777* (Philadelphia: Athenaeum of Philadelphia, 2000).

Third Street facade.

First-floor rear room.

decorative plaster work to the "front room" or "great chamber" on the second floor, thereby elevating it in importance above the room below.

In 1798 Elizabeth Powel, by then a widow, sold the house to the wealthy banker William Bingham. The house then passed through the hands of a number of private owners, and in the process lost the half of its lot which Stedman had not built on and which was planted as a garden. In 1904 the Powel House passed into the hands of a dealer in "Russian and Siberian Horse Hair and Bristles" named Wolf

Klebansky. It was under Klebansky's ownership that parts of the interior were sold to the Metropolitan Museum of Art in New York and to the Philadelphia Museum of Art. When Klebanksy threatened, in 1931, to sell the house so that it could be demolished to build a parking garage, Frances Anne Wister formed a group to save and restore it. The group would later become the Philadelphia Society for the Preservation of Landmarks, the organization that continues to operate the Samuel Powel House as a museum.[2]

2. George B. Tatum, *Philadelphia Georgian: The City House of Samuel Powel* (Middletown, CT: Wesleyan University Press, 1976); T. Kaori Kitao, "Philadelphia Row House," *Swarthmore College Bulletin* (1977): 6–11.

Entrance passage.

Second-floor music room.

Detail of plaster ceiling in music room.

Rear elevation.

Robert Alexander House

Washington, D.C.

ca. 1803 ★

Capitol Hill is one of a number of Washington, D.C. neighborhoods that are defined by their rowhouses. Nonetheless, in 1893, Teunis S. Hamlin felt compelled to remind the readers of *Scribner's* that Washington was as important for its houses as for its public buildings: "[N]o other city on this continent is so rich in historical associations, and these associations are in the homes of the capital." While Capitol Hill is known for rowhouses of the late nineteenth century, earlier examples recall Washington's famed Georgetown neighborhood where many streets are lined by eighteenth- and early nineteenth-century brick residences. The Robert Alexander House is noteworthy for its connection with two prominent figures in Washington's architectural world of the Early Republic.

The lot on which the house is located went through a series of owners until it was acquired at auction in 1800 for $200 by one Hugh Densley, a plasterer who had worked on the White House and the Capitol. A speculative builder, Densley sold the lot — by this time with a house on it — to Robert Alexander in 1803 for $1,000. Like Densley, Alexander was connected with the building trade. He was a plasterer who aspired to be an architect when very few designers could claim that title. Alexander was fortunate to have the support of Benjamin Henry Latrobe, a bona fide architect. For example, when Alexander ran afoul of the U.S. Navy over work he carried out on one of its buildings, Latrobe attempted to intervene on his behalf. A native Virginian, Alexander was married to another Virginian, Helen Brown, and by 1806 owned five slaves who worked in the household.

In 1807 Alexander left Washington to build the New Orleans Customs House that Latrobe had designed. He leased his house to Latrobe who lived there with his second wife and four children. Although Alexander had left town, he and Latrobe continued to collaborate on speculative investments. Latrobe made some alterations to the house, chiefly in order to create an office for himself, but left shortly after Alexander's death in the New Orleans yellow fever epidemic of 1811. After that time, the house went through a succession of owners, most of whom rented it out.

The most prominent feature of the house, which began as a rather modest three-bay house with its entrance to the street, is its two-story tower. It is likely that the tower was part of an extensive remodeling of the house that took place in 1889 under the ownership of William W. Danenhower, Jr., whose family was active in Washington, D.C. real estate development and law. Different investors rented out the house until it was sold in 1920 to William Henry Olds, the son of the founder of the Oldsmobile automobile company. The Olds family maintained the property for more than sixty years, during which Capitol Hill's fortunes fell and rose.

View from roof with the Capitol in the distance.

The tower was added after the original period of construction.

Facade.

Entrance at base of tower.

The Robert Alexander House blends elements of two important moments in its history: the Federal period when it was constructed and the late 1880s when it was altered. The original house was small and set close to the ground. The first-floor parlor still captures the original house's modest scale, as well as its Federal-period finishes. The parlor and dining room fireplace both have mantelpieces decorated by composition ornament. Often mass-produced and featuring neoclassical figures and motifs, this kind of ornament was widely used on Federal-period houses around fireplaces, doors, and windows.

The construction of the tower constituted a response to two major trends in the design of urban houses. First, the entrance tower enlarged the house and gave it a more imposing appearance in a period in which city houses were growing. Second, it was a feature of nineteenth-century Italianate style, originally developed on freestanding houses and now added to a semidetached residence. In order to incorporate this into the house, the entrance had to be moved to the side. In spite of the inconvenience, the Robert Alexander House took on a commanding appearance in its Capitol Hill neighborhood.

Stair hall.

Parlor with entrance beyond.

Dining room.

Nichols House

Boston, Massachusetts
Charles Bulfinch, Architect

The Nichols House is one of four houses built by Jonathan Mason on Beacon Hill for the eventual use of his daughters. Two of the houses — numbers 55 (the Nichols House) and 57 Mount Vernon Street — faced west and were set back from the street, while the adjoining numbers 53 and 51 were built as a row. The Nichols House has been attributed to gentleman architect Charles Bulfinch (1763–1844) and it is presumed that he designed Mason's other houses as well. Located close to the top of Beacon Hill and to the Massachusetts Statehouse, this area of Mount Vernon Street was intended, by its developers the Mount Vernon Proprietors, to be lined with freestanding mansions. However, the construction of four rowhouses on Mount Vernon Street in 1803 by Stephen Higginson established a more urban density of building that was perpetuated by Mason the following year in this group of houses.[1]

The house exteriors have the characteristics of a townhouse or rowhouse from the Federal period. The brick walls are flat and enlivened only by string courses in contrasting materials, following Georgian precedent. The distinctive design of the Nichols House comes from first-story arches, into which the windows are recessed. Thus the facade gains depth without extending the house. Inside, the major rooms are located one floor above the street-level entrance. These are the parlor, which occupies most of the front of the house, and the dining room behind it. At the mantelpiece in the parlor, the detailing is consistent with Federal-period neoclassicism. The swags above the fireplace echo a favorite Federal form in woodwork and furniture inlay.

The house is named for Rose Nichols, who preserved it as a museum, and its furnishings reflect her taste. The Nichols family moved into the house in 1885, when Rose was thirteen years old, and she spent the rest of her life in it. Rose's mother, Elizabeth Fisher Homer, was the sister-in-law of the well-known sculptor Augustus Saint-Gaudens, and it was through her uncle that Rose became interested in landscape gardening. Like Saint-Gaudens, the Nichols family summered in Cornish, New Hampshire, which was an important art colony at the turn of the century. There, Rose Nichols met the architect Charles A. Platt and was tutored by him in design. She also took courses at the Massachusetts Institute of Technology and at the Ecole des Beaux-arts in Paris. As a landscape architect, Rose Nichols was inspired by the formal garden tradition, a topic she wrote about in her first book, *English Pleasure Gardens* (1902), and in subsequent publications on European gardens. Over the course of her career, Nichols executed plans for some thirty gardens from California to New England. Many were undertaken for fellow members of Boston's social elite. Rose Nichols was also devoted to many progressive social causes that were the subjects of discussion at her famous Sunday afternoon teas, held at 55 Mount Vernon Street. Nichols promoted what she called the "Puritan point of view," that mutual understanding between diverse people would be fostered through dialogue.[2]

1. Harold Kirker, *The Architecture of Charles Bulfinch* (Cambridge, MA: Harvard University Press, 1969), 196–7.

2. Judith B. Tankard, "Rose Standish Nichols: A Proper Bostonian," *Arnoldia* (1999–2000 Winter): 25–32; George Taloumis et al., *Rose Standish Nichols as We Knew Her* (Boston: Friends of Rose Standish Nichols, 1986).

1804 ★

Narrow Mount Vernon Street facade, which is part of the fabric of Federal-period Beacon Hill.

Entry hall and stairway.

Facade overlooking a small garden.

*Parlor with many furnishings that belonged to
Rose Standish Nichols.*

Cast-iron cookstove.

*Bedroom showing examples of needlework by Rose
Standish Nichols, the occupant from 1885 to 1960.*

Dining room with sideboard.

William Hickling Prescott House

Boston, Massachusetts
Asher Benjamin, Architect

The William Hickling Prescott House, at 55 Beacon Street, and the adjoining house at 54 Beacon Street were built in 1808 for the Boston merchant James Smith Colburn. The pair occupies an important site overlooking Boston Common, below the State House, on Beacon Hill. They show how British neoclassical architecture was adapted for townhouse design in the United States, during the Early Republic. The coordinated designs treated as a single composition united by a continuous first-story porch, approached in ambition the efforts of the Adams in Great Britain and Bulfinch in America.

The house's original owner, James Colburn, was a prosperous Massachusetts-born merchant who prospered as a young man through his business partnership with Thomas Otis. The house is named, however, for its occupant from 1845 to 1859, the historian William Hickling Prescott. Born in 1796, Prescott came from a wealthy family and was educated at Harvard College and in Europe. In 1837 he published his first historical study, *Ferdinand and Isabella*, which was followed by other books on Spanish and Latin-American history, prior to his early death in 1859. When Samuel Eliot wrote about Prescott in the *New England Magazine* thirty-five years after the historian's death, it was to record the memories of those who had known him personally, rather than those who had encountered him only through his writings. Eliot particularly stressed Prescott's attachment to family homes in Boston and Pepperell, Massachusetts, and said of the house at 55 Beacon Street that "as years went by, and the house took on the wonted look of one long occupied, it ceased to be compared with any other, and fulfilled its own office as a handsome and yet wholly unostentatious residence for the owner and his family."

By the end of the nineteenth century, the Prescott House may have appeared unostentatious, but at the time of its construction it would have been understood as impressive. While the Colburn houses shared features with smaller townhouses of the period, such as brick construction and contrasting wood trim painted white, their scale and degree of finish set them above the others. The bowed sections of the facade are set off by pilasters and the doors are surmounted by fanlights. The interiors have elaborate door, window, and fireplace surrounds. As in other luxurious residences in both England and the United States, here the most important rooms are elevated to the second story above street level, sometimes referred to in the European manner as the *piano nobile*. The second-story rooms enjoy commanding views of Boston Common. Their bow fronts also make for variously shaped rooms, forms that were highly prized in the period.

Asher Benjamin (1773–1845), who probably designed Colburn's houses, was born in Hartland, Connecticut. Benjamin published the well-known *Country Builder's Assistant* (1797) and wrote seven handbooks of architecture (in forty-seven editions) between 1797 and 1856. As architectural historian Jack Quinan wrote, Benjamin "dominated the field of architectural writing for more than 50 years in America." He had training as a housewright but early in his career worked with Charles Bulfinch on the State Capitol in Hartford, Connecticut, designing and building its circular staircase. Quinan maintains that the Colburn houses demonstrate that "Benjamin had acquired a sound working knowledge of the spatial and decorative characteristics of the Roman neoclassical style in his first decade of practice." Benjamin's affinity for the oval forms can be observed in the Hartford staircase project as well as in the facades of the Colburn houses, which are among the earliest examples of Boston bow-front rowhouses.[1]

Prescott made significant changes to the house at 55 Beacon Street. A library, which was a gathering place for the literary elite during Prescott's lifetime, was included in a rear addition. The projection also contained a study on the third floor, where Prescott may have written two books, the *History of the Conquest*

1. Jack Quinan, "Introduction" to an issue on Asher Benjamin and American Architecture, *Journal of the Society of Architectural Historians*, 38, no. 3 (Oct., 1979): 244–253.

1808 ★

Beacon Street facade overlooking Boston Common.

of Peru (1847) and three volumes on *The History of the Reign of Philip II, King of Spain* (1855–1858). Following Prescott's death, the house was inhabited by his widow. It was subsequently purchased by her nephew, Franklin Gordon Dexter. The Dexter family replaced the original spiral staircase with a Colonial Revival staircase that is still in place. In 1944 the house was purchased by The National Society of the Colonial Dames of America in The Commonwealth of Massachusetts, who continues to operate it as a museum.

Colonial Revival staircase.

Entrance hall.

Bedroom.

*Parlor with furnishings donated by members of
the Colonial Dames.*

*View along Beacon Street with the William
Hickling Prescott House at center.*

Library.

Nathaniel Russell House

Charleston, South Carolina

"Probably the South's finest town house of the Federal period,"[1] the Nathaniel Russell House testifies to the city's prosperity prior to the War of 1812, and reflects its owner's conversancy with the elite architecture of American and British cities. While its setting is urban, the Russell house is surrounded by plantings. The English writer William Faux recalled the greenery in *Memorable Days in America* (1823) in which he wrote that he had "Called on the venerable Nathaniel Russell, Esq., residing in a splendid mansion surrounded by a wilderness of flowers, and bowers of myrtles, oranges, and lemons, smothered with fruit and flowers."

Nathaniel Russell, whom Faux described as "very courteous and friendly," was born in Bristol, Rhode Island, but came to Charleston in 1765 when he was just shy of thirty years old, working as a commercial agent for merchants in his home state. In 1788 he married Sarah Hopton, the daughter of a prosperous Charleston merchant. Russell helped to found and was the first president of the New England Society, a charitable organization for Charlestonians with roots in the North, which earned him the moniker of "The King of the Yankees." In 1808 Russell and his family, along with eighteen slaves, moved into the grand house he had built over the previous five years. That piece of land constituted lot number 247 of the "Grand Modell," the plan of Charleston that had guided the city's development since the late seventeenth century.

The house embodies aspects of both urban and rural houses of the Federal period. As in other Charleston examples, the shorter three-bay facade addresses the street. The brick construction contrasts with lighter-colored stone and wood trim, especially in the splayed lintels above the windows and the string course that links the lintels at the second, principal level. The importance of the second story is signaled by its taller proportions and by the iron balcony that runs below its windows. The front elevation contains an elaborate center entrance which is emphasized by Federal-style detailing: The door is surmounted by a fanlight and framed by pilasters. The most notable feature of the longer side elevation is its four-sided bay. The incorporation of various room configurations that moved beyond traditional boxiness was a hallmark of Federal-period architecture. However, the incorporation of oval and circular rooms into rectangular houses was accomplished more easily in country houses, where the masses of buildings could swell without limitations. Russell achieved this in an urban context. In suburban houses and country estates, curving or multisided bays also contributed to an integration of dwelling and landscape — such elements opened onto porches and gardens. Here the bay provides a view over the garden, and elongated second-story windows provide expansive openings onto the street.

The quintessentially Federal motif of the fanlight is carried through, just as the spatial drama of the exterior bay extends to the major spaces of the Nathaniel Russell House. The "free flying" staircase unites the interior, and because it is structurally separate from the stairhall walls, it can be extensively lit by a Palladian-style window between the first and second stories. An oval window in the stairhall above the second story echoes the curving forms of the bow and stair. In the second-story drawing or music room, the perfect symmetry of the oval space is extended through the use of false mirrored doors flanking the center entrance from the stairhall. These features create three openings to balance the three windows on the outside wall, while they also add complexity by reflecting the inhabitants of the room. On such occasions as the festivities that accompanied the 1809 marriage of Russells's eldest daughter, Alicia, to Arthur Middleton of Bolton Plantation, reflective surfaces and candlelight would have combined to create an impression of opulence.

A central feature of the Federal style was its incorporation of neoclassical motifs drawn from the work of Robert Adam, and widely published. The interior of the Russell House has many such features, including neoclassical fireplace surrounds and

1. According to Richard and Dorothy Pratt, *Second Treasury of Early American Homes* (New York: Hawthorn Books, 1954).

1808 ★

The longer garden facade has a bay, which accommodates curved interior rooms.

2. Ronald L. Hurst, "The Chesapeake" in Ronald L. Hurst and Jonathan Prown, *Southern Furniture 1680–1830: The Colonial Williamsburg Collection* (Williamsburg, VA and New York: Colonial Williamsburg Foundation and Harry N. Abrams, Inc., 1997), 30.

doors framed by pilasters. The furnishings complement the architectural style and include many objects based on classical forms. They show how wealthy Charlestonians emulated the sophisticated ways of the British, to whom they looked as role models. The refined furnishings could also be rearranged for social events, with light chairs and tables easily moved to the sides of the rooms to accommodate large groups of guests. Indeed, by the second decade of the nineteenth century, entertaining was important to Charleston's elite who had retreated "into a genteel and select clique bound by common ancestry, inherited wealth, and a shared passion for the cultured pastimes of balls, musicales, and tea parties."[2]

After decades of private ownership, the Nathaniel Russell House served, after the Civil War, as the mother house of an order of Catholic nuns and a school. In 1955 it was acquired by the Historic Charleston Foundation and was a symbol of the early preservation movement in the city. By the mid-twentieth century Charleston — despite its loss as a commercial center — became celebrated for its architecture. The "unique glimpse of a particular kind of early American architecture," which Charleston became known for, was not only due to superb individual monuments like the Nathaniel Russell House, but also to the ensemble of buildings. As Frederic L. Stevenson and Carl Feiss wrote in 1951, "The memory of that glimpse is not one of individually attractive buildings but rather of groups of buildings: street pictures of a townscape more harmonious than is usual even in the older American cities."

Detail of drawing room woodwork.

Second-story drawing room furnished in the neo-classical taste. The curving wall is reflected in the bay on the exterior.

First-story entrance hall.

Stair hall.

Dining room with the hallway beyond.

Narrow three-bay facade facing the street.

Francis Stone House

Savannah, Georgia

Completed in 1817, this house was built for Francis Stone, a Savannah alderman who was known as a hero of the 1854 yellow fever epidemic. Wood-framed and close to the street, the Stone House typifies Savannah townhouses of the Federal period and reflects a time of rapid urban growth.

Laid out at the behest of King George II in 1733 by General James Oglethorpe, Savannah's plan was distinguished by its grid pattern, "delightfully relieved by twenty-four squares, most of which comprise embowered oases." Rapid population growth led to the expansion of the original grid; the blocks surrounding Columbia Square where the Francis Stone House is located were laid out in 1799. Around 1800 the squares were landscaped as parks. Blessed with a good port on the Savannah River, the city prospered, especially through the export of Sea Island cotton. Much rebuilding followed a massive fire in 1796 that destroyed more than 200 buildings. A second fire in 1820 caused twice the damage but did not dampen Savannah's economic growth during its "Golden Age" following the end of the War of 1812. In 1839 English visitor James Silk Buckingham observed that, "The greater number of the dwelling houses are built of wood, and painted white; but there are many handsome and commodious brick buildings occupied as private residences, and a few mansions…"[1] The Englishman Adam Hodgson had argued earlier that persisting with wood-framed construction in the wake of the fires was a mistake. He wrote in 1824 that, "The traveler, in passing, enters his protest against the doings of the people of Savannah, who were so unwise as to build wooden houses on the ruins of those lately burnt down."

The Francis Stone House was a frame house and it also corresponds to the first group of houses Buckingham identified. A city house, it is sited close to the street, allowing for a yard at the back of the property. The detailing is relatively simple both on the exterior, where the entrance is sheltered by a columned porch, and on the interior, where the fireplaces are framed with flat-board surrounds. The facade evidences a somewhat unusual plan in that it possesses four bays rather than the expected three, likely as a result of a remodeling that took place in 1880. A window located to the right of the front door lights a large entrance hall, a feature which could not have been accommodated in the original house.

Like many other Savannah houses, the Francis Stone House fell into disrepair in the early twentieth century as the city's economic fortunes declined. Yet the house later became part of the story of Savannah's rehabilitation. In 1927 it was purchased by preservationist Fred Wessels, Jr., who leased it in 1958 to the Historic Savannah Foundation, Inc., the preservation organization which had been chartered in 1955. The Stone House was subsequently restored by Mills B. Lane IV, a publisher and philanthropist who funded the preservation of many Savannah houses. By the early 1970s, *Southern Living* could sing the praises of "walled and green Savannah" where "The walls are houses and buildings that closely line its streets. The green reaches out over the sidewalks and unfolds beautifully in square after square across the old town."

1. Turpin C. Bannister, "Oglethorpe's Sources for the Savannah Plan," *Journal of the Society of Architectural Historians*, 20, no. 2 (May, 1961): 47–56; Page Talbott, *Classical Savannah: Fine & Decorative Arts 1800–1840* (Savannah, Georgia: Telfair Museum of Art, 1995).

1817 ★

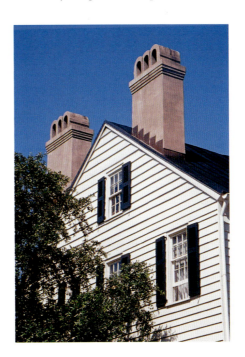

Gable detail.

Front elevation.

Stairway from front entrance.

opposite, top: First-floor parlor, or living room.

opposite, bottom: Bedroom.

Rear porch.

Rear yard made possible by close placement of the house to the street.

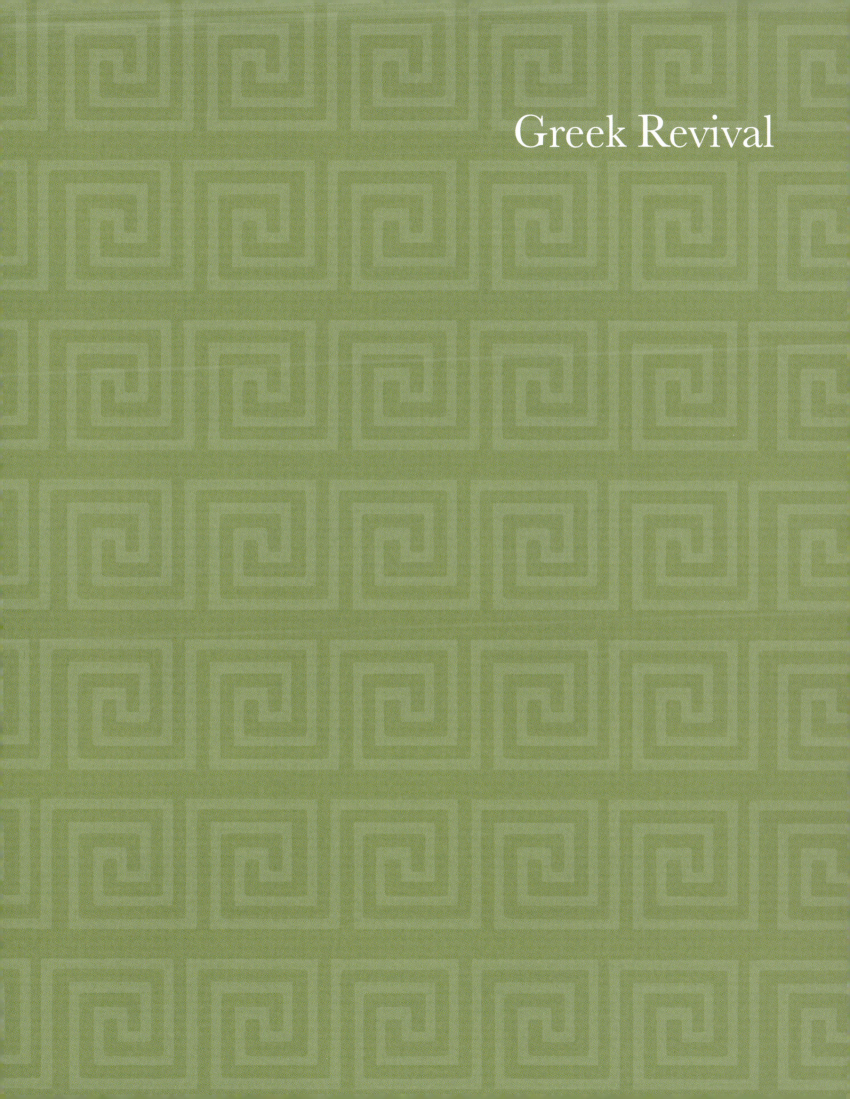

Greek Revival

Merchant's House Museum

New York City

A "fly in amber" is how architecture critic Ada Louise Huxtable characterized the Merchant's House Museum at 29 East Fourth Street in Manhattan. Built on speculation around 1831, by a hatter named Joseph Brewster, the house was purchased in 1835 by merchant Seabury Tredwell. It represents the transition from the Federal to the Greek Revival style and preserves many of the interior treatments and furnishings associated with the Tredwell family.[1] According to historian Talbot Hamlin, the house gives a sense of how the rooms of the Greek Revival rowhouses of the affluent were furnished and lived in: "[I]t illustrates how harmoniously the simple mahogany surfaces and the rather heavy carving of the so-called American Empire furniture, relieved here and there by the lighter pieces of Duncan Phyfe or his followers, resting on rich French carpets, fitted into those tall and ample rooms."

The three-and-one-half story brick facade with contrasting stone and wood trim recalls rowhouses of the eighteenth and early nineteenth centuries. However, certain elements of the ornament suggest the emergence of the Greek Revival style as a favored idiom for domestic architecture. So refined are some of the features of the Merchant's House, that they have been compared to details published by Minard Lafever (1798–1854) in *The Beauties of Modern Architecture* (1835), *The Young Builder's General Instructor* (1829), and *The Modern Builder's Guide* (1833). Lafever's publications followed the model of Asher Benjamin's in providing usable designs for builders in places that lacked professional architects, but developed a more overtly Greek-inspired idiom, in contrast to the Palladian neoclassicism of Benjamin's designs. In addition to the quality of the design, Hamlin praises the execution of the work: "The [Merchant's] house shows too, in the exquisiteness of its carving (the main floor newel with its sweeping acanthus scroll at the bottom of the handrail is characteristic) and in the grace of its exterior railings, the high standards of workmanship then current." The transitional nature of the house, illustrating the

development from the Federal to Greek Revival styles, is particularly evident in the main doorway over which the fanlight is supported by Ionic columns. Fully disengaged from the door frame, these columns anticipate the sculptural use of the orders of the late Greek Revival style. Tredwell's cousin's house (Skidmore House, 1844–45), three lots east, had Ionic columns that framed the doorway but not recessed into the facade (as they are at the Merchant's House), rather they are pulled entirely free to sit in front of the wall.

The interior of the Merchant's House is entirely consistent with the early Greek Revival New York townhouse. On the first floor, the side hall opens onto back-to-back double parlors separated by Ionic columns. Although the rear parlor is now set up as a dining room, there was an everyday dining room

Facade.

1. Lewis Iman Sharp, "The Old Merchant's House: An 1831/32 New York Row House," M.A. Thesis, University of Delaware, 1968.

Detail of surround on front entrance.

Entrance hall with stair.

Dormer detail.

on the lower level, as well as a kitchen, which had access to the small rear yard. The arrangement of the first story with two main rooms was carried through to the second story where there are two principal bedrooms and a smaller room over the front entrance. Between the two main chambers are fitted closets with drawers for clothes. Above the second floor, the scale and finishes of the spaces diminish and may have been used for family or servant bedrooms. Off the rear of the main block, as was common in the period, was a wood-frame ell, or "tea room." This room was a response to a perceived need for additional space in the conventional rowhouse, as it was further developed in later examples to create a house that was fully three rooms deep. In the later Skidmore House, which is in many respects very similar to the Merchant's House, the plan of the main floor is a full three rooms deep with a substantial projection to the rear.

When critic Montgomery Schuyler published a view of the Old Merchant's House in the *Architectural Record* in 1899, it still adjoined a similar house at number 27 East Fourth Street, which has since been demolished. With at least one other member of the original row, the Merchant's House illustrated more fully how the repetitive form of the rowhouse facade was used to create a unified streetscape in the areas of Manhattan that were developed for housing after 1825. Over time, the Merchant's House became more of an anomaly and only the fact that it remained in the hands of descendants of its second owner until the 1930s ensured its preservation. By 1964 Huxtable could write that the Merchant's House was "sadly in need of maintenance in a neighborhood that has gone steadily downhill. (This is now the fringe of the old-bum-and-broken-bottle territory.)" Visitors today would be shocked by Huxtable's characterization, both because the house has been carefully maintained by the Merchant's House Museum and the Historic House Trust of New York City, and because its neighborhood — still gritty and marked by a diversity of residential and commercial uses — has become a desirable residential area once more.

Rear parlor on main floor with columns separating it from the front parlor reflected in the pier mirror.

Bedroom.

Kitchen on lower level.

Andrew S. Norwood House

New York City

This house demonstrates the grandeur that could be achieved in the design of an attached house while keeping to the standard three-bay formula. It also reflects the spread of residential development in Manhattan during the mid-1840s and the stylistic transformations that accompanied it.

The builder of the house, financier Andrew S. Norwood, was a prosperous partner in the firm of Norwood and Austin which lent money to the federal government during the War of 1812. The Norwood family was described as being "among the oldest of the Knickerbockers upon this island." Both the location and scale of the house demonstrated the owner's wealth and social standing. At the time the house was constructed, it was on the edge of Manhattan's northward development. As historian Dell Upton describes, beginning in the 1820s, the merchants who were then profiting from the commercial activity around the port at the southern end of Manhattan Island "began to move away from their waterfront stores and residences." On the west side and center section of the island, merchant families erected houses in Greenwich Village near Washington Square, Astor Place, and Union Square and after the mid-1840s "up Fifth Avenue, the hotbed of the 'Codfish Aristocracy,' as the new rich were called."[1] The street on which Norwood built his house was a particularly wide cross-town thoroughfare on the border between Greenwich Village and Chelsea, which was eventually lined with large townhouses. This house was originally one of a group of three built for Norwood. At thirty feet wide, it fit the scale of the street, which was considerably more ample than the standard brownstone.

Indeed, the Norwood House is nearly twice as wide as the Italianate rowhouses of the third quarter of the nineteenth century. The Norwood house occupies a position between the Greek Revival and the Italianate. It is constructed of brick like many earlier houses, but sports rusticated brownstone at the basement level, the classical door enframement, and the window surrounds and lintels. In keeping with the Italianate spirit, the first story windows are elongated into French windows that open onto iron balconies.

The elegance of the interior of the Norwood House derives first from its scale; the entrance hall, for example, is ten feet wide. Moreover, to compensate for the cramped entry area, the staircase is in this instance reversed. With the steps rising from the rear of the hall, the entry becomes more spacious. The staircase is lit from above by a stained-glass skylight. Otherwise, the plan recalls earlier rowhouses, with double parlors on the first floor connected by a

Detail of front entrance surround with neoclassical elements in brownstone contrasting with brick facade.

1. Dell Upton, "Inventing the Metropolis: Civilization and Urbanity," in Catherine Hoover Voorsanger and John J. Howat, eds., *Art and the Empire City: New York, 1825–1861* (New York: The Metropolitan Museum of Art; New Haven and London: Yale University Press, 2000), 15–17.

2. Charles Lockwood, "The Rescue and Restoration of a New York City Landmark," *The Magazine Antiques* (January 2004): 160–169.

1845–47 ▣

Front elevation.

Entrance hall with stair rising from the rear.

Second-story room above entrance.

large opening with pocket doors. The framing elements around the door and window openings are classical, in keeping with the Greek Revival style, but the elaborately carved stair elements and bold ceiling moldings reflect the emerging Italianate sensibility. An elaborate stone mantelpiece in the front parlor is also representative of mid-century tastes. The dimensions of the Norwood House allow for the expansion of the usual accompaniment of rooms on the upper floors. Above the entry, for example, a smaller room, flanking the front bedroom, was introduced.

Following the death of Andrew S. Norwood in 1856, the house was inherited by his son, Andrew G. Norwood, who like his father was a prosperous businessman. The house remained in the Norwood family into the twentieth century even as the neighborhood around it declined.[2] Already by the end of the nineteenth century, newly developed neighborhoods farther uptown were surpassing lower Manhattan in

desirability. The wider streets of Greenwich Village and other downtown neighborhoods witnessed their earlier houses giving way to commercial enterprises and to apartment buildings. Although Greenwich Village enjoyed notoriety in the early twentieth century as a bohemian enclave, by 1950 it had lost some of its cachet. As Eleanor Early wrote in her popular travel book, *New York Holiday* (1950), "Greenwich Village is a fascinating place, but it is not Bohemia any more. Some of it is 'arty' and much of it is charming. But it is not the mad and wonderful place it used to be." By the time that the Norwood House was completely renovated in the late 1970s, its location was considered to be (in the words of its owner) "offbeat" and a somewhat derelict setting for so grand a house. The ensuing decades have, however, witnessed a complete turn-around in the neighborhood's desirability, in part due to the renovation of its extensive collection of nineteenth-century houses.

Front parlor.

Bedroom with four-poster bed made in New York around 1830.

Dining room.

Henry Willink Houses

Savannah, Georgia

These mirror-image houses were built for Henry F. Willink, an owner of the prominent Savannah Willink & Miller shipyard and a city alderman. During the Civil War Willink produced the armored vessels "Savannah" and "Milledgeville," as well as the gunboat "Macon." Like other shipyards throughout the South, his prospered from the Confederate Navy's reliance on private enterprises for vessels.[1] The CSS "Savannah," an ironclad steam sloop built in 1863, was considered one of the finest vessels in the Confederate naval squadron. She was burned on the Savannah River by the Confederates on December 21, 1864, as General W. T. Sherman approached the city.

The pair of houses were probably built as rental properties to capitalize on the influx of workers who were drawn to Savannah in the 1850s by the economic activity associated with the cotton trade. Transportation from the interior of Georgia to the port was facilitated by the completion, in 1843, of the Central of Georgia Railroad line that linked Macon and Savannah. The introduction of steamships on the Savannah River in the 1840s also increased activity in the city. By 1860 Savannah had become the largest city in Georgia, with more than 22,000 residents — including its nearly 8,000 slaves.

The growing population was accommodated by houses of varying sophistication and size, including several types of townhouses. The neoclassical style was popularized around 1820 by William Jay III (1792–1837), an architect who had come to Savannah from Bath, England. He designed the Owens-Thomas House (1819) and others for members of Savannah's elite, which incorporated elements of classical architecture.[2] Later Savannah architects perpetuated the use of classical forms and specifically adopted Greek-inspired columns for townhouses. The designer of the Willink Houses modified an earlier form of attached urban house and updated it with certain Greek Revival elements. Like Federal-period rows, the Willink Houses are two-and-a-half stories above a raised basement. Although the steeply pitched roof punctuated by dormers was an eighteenth-century formula, the door surrounds of the house were more contemporary. They are surmounted by transoms and flanked by long sidelights that are characteristic of the Greek Revival style.

Inside, on the main level, the stairhall provides access to two connected parlors, each with its own fireplace. These are vented through a massive center chimney that recalls eighteenth-century architecture. In keeping with the modest Greek Revival character of the houses, their interior finishes are subdued and include pilastered chimney pieces.

1. William N. Still, Jr., "Facilities for the Construction of War Vessels in the Confederacy," *The Journal of Southern History* 31, no. 3 (Aug., 1965): 285–304.

2. Page Talbott, *Classical Savannah: Fine & Decorative Arts 1800–1840* (Savannah: Telfair Museum of Art, 1995).

1850

Entrance to one of the houses.

The two mirror-image facades.

Entrance hall.

View from dining room to parlor.

Front parlor.

Rear garden.

Bedroom.

Entrance hall.

Facade of house on right.

Front parlor.

Dining room with parlor beyond.

Bedroom.

Rear garden.

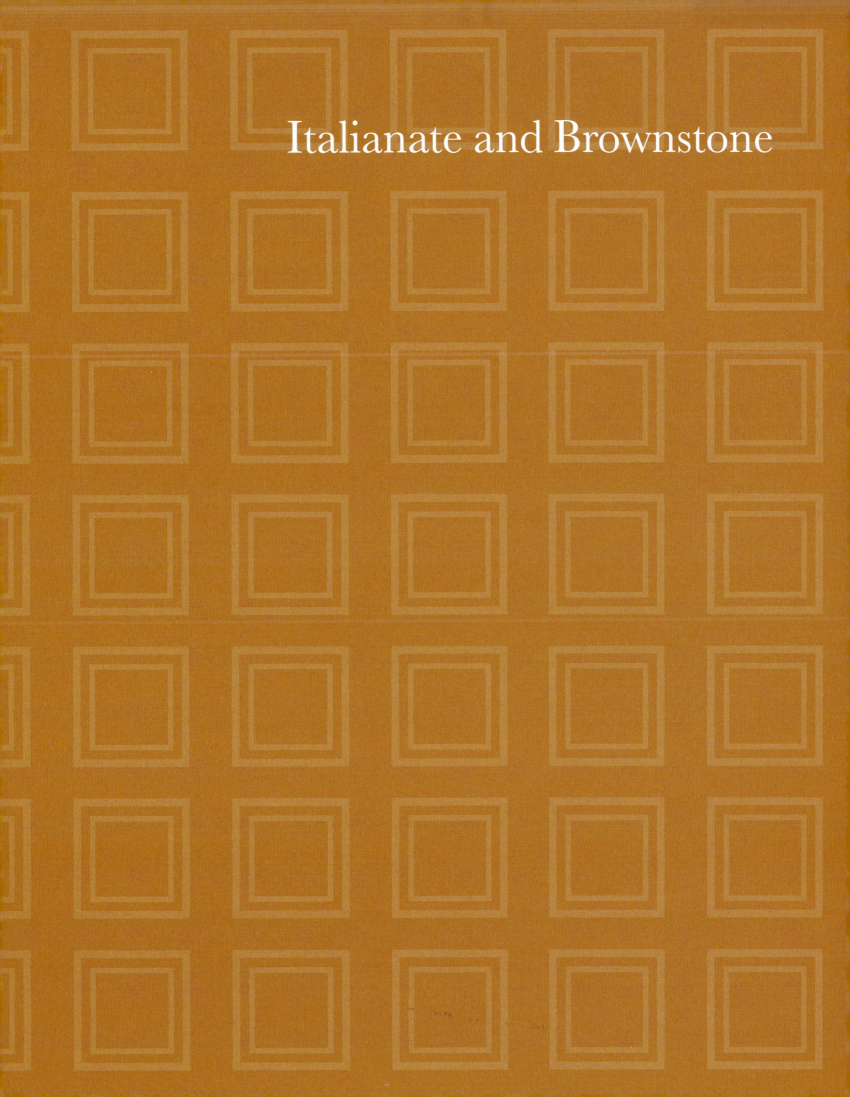

Italianate and Brownstone

Theodore Roosevelt Birthplace

New York City

Theodate Pope Riddle, Architect (1923 Reconstruction)

Although the existing Theodore Roosevelt Birthplace is a reconstruction, it reflects the original appearance of the late-1840s rowhouse. Its historical associations make the building an important one, but it also represents a fairly rare treatment of a brownstone front since it possesses certain medieval details that were part of the Romantic historicism of the middle decades of the nineteenth century.

The house was built in 1848 and purchased by Theodore's grandfather, Cornelius Van Schaack Roosevelt, in 1854, as a wedding gift for the youngest of his five sons, Theodore Roosevelt, Sr., and his wife, Martha Bulloch. The adjoining house at number 26 was purchased for Theodore Sr.'s brother Robert. Theodore Roosevelt was born at 28 East 20th Street in 1858 and lived there until 1872. He studied at Harvard College between 1876 and 1880 and, shortly after graduating, married Alice Hathaway Lee of Massachusetts and joined the Republican party. Roosevelt's first political victory was election to the New York State Assembly in 1881. In 1884, his first child, Alice Lee Roosevelt, was born, but her mother died within days from Bright's disease. Two years later, Roosevelt married Edith Kermit Carow and the couple had their first child shortly thereafter. During the 1880s and 1890s Roosevelt published a number of books while his family continued to grow, and he pursued his political career. During the Spanish-American War, Roosevelt served with the "Rough Riders" (the First U.S. Volunteer Cavalry Regiment), rising to the rank of Colonel before the Battle of San Juan Heights. Soon after the war, in 1898, Roosevelt was elected Governor of New York, a position he held until 1900. The following year he was elected Vice President of the United States, but he became the youngest President in history (at age forty-two) when President William McKinley was shot in September of that year. Roosevelt's presidency, which lasted until 1909, brought about a number of important reforms, including antitrust suits and the establishment of the National Forest Service. In 1906 Roosevelt was awarded the Nobel Peace Prize for his role in mediating the end to the Russo-Japanese War. After his presidency, Roosevelt continued to pursue a diplomatic and political career, and to cultivate his interests in writing and sportsmanship, until his death in 1919.

Theodore Roosevelt died just three years after his birthplace had been demolished and replaced by a modest commercial building. Within days of his death, the Roosevelt Memorial Association was established. The group joined with the Women's Roosevelt Memorial Association to reconstruct the President's birthplace, with the support of Roosevelt's widow and daughters. The Robert Roosevelt House was demolished to make way for offices and other functions related to a house museum. The reconstruction of the Theodore Roosevelt Birthplace was completed in three years and opened to the public in October 27, 1923, which would have been the former president's sixty-fifth birthday.[1]

The architect in charge of the project was Theodate Pope Riddle (1867–1946) who had trained informally with the firm of McKim, Mead and White while they built her parents' home, Hillstead, in Farmington, Connecticut (1898–1901). Riddle became a licensed architect in New York state in 1916 and maintained a professional office in New York city until 1924. Her reconstruction of the Roosevelt Birthplace was dependent on the recollections of two of the President's younger sisters as well as his widow, who had visited the house as a child. Detailed recollections of the house's redecoration by the firm of Léon Marcotte made it possible for Riddle and the Woman's Roosevelt Memorial Association to restore the interior to its 1865 appearance. While the effort to restore and furnish the house was meticulous, in ensuing years, the original installation was compromised by inappropriate alterations and general wear. When the Theodore Roosevelt Birthplace was acquired by the National Park Service in 1963, it needed another restoration, which came about in 1976.

1. David M. Kahn, "The Theodore Roosevelt Birthplace in New York City," *The Magazine Antiques* 116 (July 1979): 176–181; Charles B. Hosmer, Jr., *The Presence of the Past: A History of the Preservation Movement in the United States Before Williamsburg* (New York: G.P. Putnam's Sons, 1965), 147–152.

1848 ■

Front elevation.

Parlor.

Library.

The exterior recreates the appearance of a mid-nineteenth century brownstone approached from the street by a high stoop. What is unique about the facade are the medieval touches, including the Tudor-style molding above the front door. The reconstructed house shows that the Roosevelts had the usual number of rooms that any large urban rowhouse in New York City possessed then. The family used the rooms, as did their peers, reserving the parlor for the most formal occasions. As Theodore Roosevelt recalled the parlor in his *Autobiography* (1913), "[It was] a room of much splendor…open for general use only on Sunday evening or on rare occasions when there was a party." With its marble mantelpiece, enormous pier mirror, deeply-tufted furniture, and glittering chandelier, the parlor epitomizes the mid-century aesthetic that the Theodore Roosevelt Birthplace has been recreated to represent.

Mr. and Mrs. Roosevelt's bedroom.

The bedroom of young "Teedie," as he was called as a child.

Dining room.

Isaac Van Anden House

Brooklyn, New York

"On or near the Heights chiefly dwelt the small, refined, and very exclusive society then dominant in Brooklyn. These heights, notwithstanding their raggedness, formed, I believe, the noblest promenade in the world, and, I am sure, one of the most beautiful." So Richard Grant White described in *The Century* magazine in 1883 the appearance in earlier days of what would become one of New York's finest neighborhoods of townhouses. The extensive construction of attached houses in Brooklyn Heights at the middle of the nineteenth century — which White called its "hideous and deplorable transformation" — actually resulted in streets lined by fine residences in a variety of styles then considered up-to-date. This Italianate house is part of a row constructed in the 1850s to take advantage of commanding views over the East River to Manhattan.

The establishment of a steam ferry between lower Manhattan and Brooklyn Heights in 1814 inaugurated the neighborhood's development as a residential suburb of New York City. In 1807 there had been only seven houses in Brooklyn Heights and a cluster of twenty additional buildings near the river. In the massive building campaign that followed, rowhouses predominated, although there were scattered developments of fully detached houses. Nearby, on Columbia Heights, stood one of the finest groups of attached houses in the Greek Revival style. The Colonnade Row, which consisted of eight four-story brick houses fronted by a continuous colonnade, was built before 1840 but destroyed by fire in 1853. After the middle of the century, rowhouses continued to be built in a variety of historicist styles.

The first modern historian of Brooklyn Heights's architecture, Clay Lancaster, identified this house and its immediate neighbors as some of the finest examples of the Renaissance Revival style, a variation on the Italianate. Lancaster cites characteristics of the style evident in this house: the use of brown-stone, increased height, "and an abundance of ornamentation, especially around openings. Some of these features, such as capitals, friezes and consoles, are embellished with lush carvings of acanthus leaves and less orthodox forms of vegetation." The house also exhibits other features associated with the Renaissance Revival style, including massive balusters in place of thin railings at the front steps, bold lintels at the windows and doors, and an entranceway that is recessed from the facade.[1]

The interior follows some of the basic elements of the earlier Greek Revival rowhouses but the scale of the building is perceptibly expanded. The ceilings soar and the side entrance hall is of ample width. The bay at the rear expands the depth of the house, offering views over the Brooklyn Heights Promenade.

1. Clay Lancaster, *Old Brooklyn Heights: New York's First Suburb*, 2d ed. (Mineola, NY: Dover Publications, 1979), 67–72.

ca. 1855

Detail of brownstone door hood.

Brownstone row.

In some Italianate rowhouses, the familiar Greek-Revival plan, with two main rooms and a "tea room" extension off of the rear of the parlor level, was expanded to three large rooms. To conform to the larger scale of the Italianate rowhouse (in comparison to the Greek Revival), the size of the decorative elements was also increased. Fireplace surrounds, ceiling moldings, and door and window trim were all boldly scaled.

The house was an appropriate residence for its best-known occupant, Isaac Van Anden, the owner of the *Brooklyn Eagle* newspaper. (Van Anden had founded the daily in 1841 with Henry Cruse Murphy.) Around 1863, Van Anden moved into the already-constructed house, and he would live there for the rest of his life. In 1875, Van Anden was eulogized as an "all over Brooklyn man" who had contributed to the city in many ways, including holding various public offices and contributing $25,000 to the construction of the Brooklyn Bridge. Today, Van Anden is remembered for having fired poet Walt Whitman as editor of the *Brooklyn Eagle* over a political disagreement. Van Anden was unmarried but presumably required such a large house as an expression of his high standing in the community.

Brooklyn Heights' rowhouse district fluctuated in popularity, just like many other urban neighborhoods in New York. In 1893 Julian Ralph wrote in *Harper's* that "The oldest Brooklyn houses on the Heights are of brick and brownstone, like our own on Manhattan. They are becoming boarding houses now, for the Heights district is not what it was in days of yore." The decline of the building fabric continued into the twentieth century until 1965, when Brooklyn Heights was listed on the National Register of Historic Places and as an Historic District under New York City's Landmarks Preservation Law. After that time, the neighborhood witnessed the renovation of many of its nineteenth-century townhouses, and its desirability as a residential area near to Manhattan grew.

View up through stair.

Entrance hall.

Mantelpiece.

Dining room.

Facade detail.

View of rear from Brooklyn Heights esplanade.

Gibson House

Boston, Massachusetts
Edward Clarke Cabot, Architect

The Gibson House was one of a pair of Beacon Street houses designed by architect Edward Clarke Cabot (1818–1901) in 1860; one house was for the widow Catherine Hammond Gibson and her son Charles Hammond Gibson, and the other for a relative, S. H. Russell. The Gibson and Russell houses were the first to be constructed on the recently filled "New Land" in the Back Bay neighborhood west of Arlington Street, and they sat alone on their block for ten years. In building their house, the Gibsons took the risk that the new area would become one of the more fashionable residential sections of Boston, as it did, surpassing the adjacent South End.

Cabot was a member of a rich and influential Boston family, and he had won the 1846 architectural competition to design a new facility for the Boston Athenaeum with a Palladian design. It was surprisingly sophisticated for somebody who had had no artistic or architectural training and who had eschewed the Grand Tour for sheep-raising in Illinois and farming in Vermont. The use of Italianate forms and brownstone for the Athenaeum legitimized similar treatments for the later rowhouse fronts he designed, including the Gibson House.

Cabot designed a number of Back Bay houses in which he adapted mid- to late-nineteenth century historicist styles, both as an independent practitioner and in partnership with Francis Ward Chandler (1844–1926) from 1874–75 to 1888.[1] In the Gibson House, Cabot transformed the rowhouse plan of Beacon Hill and the South End. The common side hall arrangement of the first floor had two drawbacks, one aesthetic and the other social. First, it necessitated a straight run of steps. Second, if the hall was to serve as a transitional space between the house and the outside world, in which potential callers could be screened, then a separate vestibule had to be created while still leaving room for the stairs.

In the Gibson House these defects are compensated for by the greatly expanded stair hall, reflected on the exterior by the center entrance. In fact, although it is about the width of a rowhouse, the Gibson House

is treated more like a townhouse. Cabot divides the plan roughly in half and dedicates the space in front entirely to the entrance hall. The advantage of this plan over the side hall plan is that the stair hall is spacious and the staircase itself is set off to one side and gently curved. The devotion of such a large space in a rowhouse to a stairhall anticipates the emergence, in the next decade, of the living hall — a feature of the Queen Anne style. Early in his years as president of the Boston Society of Architects, which lasted from 1867 to 1896, Cabot presided over extended discussions about the value of the Queen Anne and its relevance in America. The major living spaces, the music room and the library, are located on the second story. Their importance is signaled by their oriel windows, ample dimensions, and high ceilings. Upper floors were devoted to family and servant bedrooms.

The Gibson House represented a departure from earlier townhouses and rowhouses, not only with respect to its plan, but also in its exterior. Cabot blends brick and brownstone, using the latter material sparingly to emphasize the street-level entrance. In the upper stories he avoids repeating patterns of window openings, but relates the different windows by using similar arched lintels at various levels. The lintels, as well as some of the other exterior details, recall the Italian Renaissance style that he had used in the design for the Boston Athenaeum.

Streetscape view.

1. Joseph M. Siry, "The Architecture of Cabot and Chandler" (Harvard University, Cambridge, MA, 1981), typescript, Boston Public Library, Fine Arts Dept.; Cynthia Slautterback, *Designing the Boston Athenaeum* (Boston, MA: The Boston Athenaeum, 1999).

1859–60 ■

Beacon Street facade.

Detail of entrance showing use of brownstone at first story.

The Gibson House now reflects the ways in which several generations of family members furnished and altered it through the early twentieth century. In 1871 Charles Gibson married Rosamond Warren who, after the death of her mother-in-law in 1888, redecorated parts of the house. Some of the dark woodwork, which by the late 1880s was becoming unfashionable, was painted over white. Preserving the house and its collection of mid-nineteenth century fine and decorative arts was the vision of Charles and Rosamond Gibson's son, Charles Jr. Known in Boston as a writer and traveler, as well as an "eccentric" and "bon vivant," Charles Gibson Jr. began to think of the house as a museum in 1936, well before his death in 1954. In 1957 the Gibson House opened to the public. Not only does the house show the furnishings of a fine Victorian residence, but it also preserves the service areas and technological gadgetry that attended the transformation of the American home at the middle of the nineteenth century.

Music room as redecorated by Rosamond Warren Gibson in the 1890s.

Entrance hall with main stair.

Dining room located on the first floor.

Kitchen with 1884 cast-iron range used by some of the seven servants, most of whom were Irish immigrants, in residence in the 1880s.

Third-floor bathroom with fixtures dating to 1902.

George and Kate Frick House

Baltimore, Maryland

Built around 1860, the house epitomizes the large Italianate rowhouses of the Bolton Hill neighborhood in the middle of the nineteenth century. Its soaring ceilings and elaborate decorative treatment indicate that it was built for an affluent buyer, in a city which offered rowhouses at every point on the economic scale.

Bolton Hill was named for the estate "Bolton" which was built by George Grundy, a British merchant who came to Baltimore in the late eighteenth century. It stood until 1900. The heart of the neighborhood, Bolton Street, where this house is located, was laid out in 1848, but most of the residential building took place after the Civil War. A few detached villas set on large lots reflect the earlier period of building on Bolton Hill. The Bolton Street trolley line encouraged development along its path in the 1880s; the nearby Bolton Station (later replaced by the Mount Vernon train station) offered other convenient transportation alternatives. While well connected to the rest of the city and beyond, Bolton Hill offered a degree of detachment from Baltimore's commercial center as well as views of the city and harbor.

The property on which the house stands might have been purchased by George Frick's parents soon after Bolton Street was laid out. George and Kate Frick were married in 1855 and in residence in the house by 1860. George Frick was a merchant of some means, and his house accommodated the family's several children and servants while at the same time expressing the family's economic position.

The house is typical of the larger Italianate rowhouses constructed in Baltimore at the middle of the nineteenth century. Despite the scale of the rooms, particularly on the parlor floor, the side hall arrangement is maintained from earlier styles. In the typical large Italianate house, the relatively narrow hallway provided access to several large rooms. This example, built on a corner lot, avoids the usual problem of the dark center of the plan, with a bay rising the full three stories, looking out onto the side street. Many Baltimore neighborhoods saw the construction of large three-story Italianate houses on the wider main thoroughfares and smaller versions with details that echoed the more expensive houses on the side streets. Thus a single neighborhood like Bolton Hill could encompass a range of housing alternatives.[1] The relative luxuriousness of this house is marked by its plaster decoration at the ceilings, marble mantelpieces, and elaborate gilt pier mirrors between the front windows and over the fireplaces.

Critic Russell Sturgis considered the mid-century Baltimore rowhouse to be superior in many ways to the typical attached New York residence of the same period. Sturgis found these city houses to be "more nearly approaching the suburban type" as a result of what he thought were the relatively lower costs of land compared to Northeast cities. In contrast to New York, the houses were set closer to the street level. In plan, this house is similar to that of a Richmond, Virginia, house illustrated by Sturgis — with a sidehall giving access to a parlor, library, dining room, and kitchen lined up one behind the other — which Sturgis praises for its "convenience and pleasantness."

1. Mary Ellen Hayward and Charles Belfoure, *The Baltimore Rowhouse* (New York: Princeton Architectural Press, 1999).

ca. 1860 ■

Front and side facades.

Sitting room.

Entrance.

Sitting room.

Parlor with pier mirror between the long
Italianate-style windows.

Bedroom.

Stair hall.

Mary McLeod Bethune House

Washington, D.C.

This house is a typical construction of the late nineteenth century, heavily influenced by the Italianate and French Second Empire styles. In the decades following the Civil War, the Logan Circle neighborhood was developed as an upper-middle class residential area, filled with speculatively built single-family houses. Although Logan Circle (formerly Iowa Circle) itself was part of the original plan of Washington, D.C., the area was not built until about 1875. During those years, houses were constructed around the circular park created by the intersection of streets designated by numbers and letters with the overlying avenues named for states (in this case Rhode Island and Vermont).

The house was built in 1875 by tobacco merchant and real estate developer William S. Roose. The previous year he had bought several lots on the south side of Vermont Avenue; the Bethune House is one of a pair he constructed on speculation. As the Historic American Building Survey notes, Logan Circle was at "its peak of popularity in the 1870s and early 1880s," when well-known figures like the son of President Ulysses S. Grant constructed massive townhouses in the area. Roose sold the house he had built at 1318 Vermont Avenue. in the same year it was finished to John J. McElhone, a reporter in the House of Representatives. McElhone lived in the house with his wife, children, and servants, and it was later occupied by a succession of owners and tenants during the decades in which Logan Circle went from being a neighborhood of single-family residences inhabited by upper-middle class white families and their servants, to one that was more densely populated with a diverse population. After the election of Franklin Delano Roosevelt the Logan Circle area became popular with African American professionals, who constituted more than half of the neighborhood's population by the 1940s.

The demographics of the neighborhood were likely one of the factors that attracted Mary McLeod Bethune to Logan Circle. In 1943 she purchased the house to serve as the headquarters of her organization, the National Council of Negro Women, and as her own residence. At the time that Mary McLeod Bethune purchased the house, she had already served for many years as president of Bethune-Cookman College in Daytona, Florida. In 1923 the college had grown out of the school for African-American girls Bethune had founded in 1904. She was appointed by President Franklin Delano Roosevelt to be director of the Division of Negro Affairs of the National Youth Administration between 1936 and 1943, making her the first African-American woman to head a federal agency. By relocating to Washington, D.C., Bethune took on a significant national role in the Civil Rights movement. As president of the National Council of Negro Women, Bethune campaigned against segregation and discrimination. Near the end of her life in 1955, *Ebony* magazine called Bethune the "First Lady of Black America"; she subsequently became known as the most influential African American woman in American history.

The Bethune House, or the Council House, as it was then known, was substantially modernized when it was acquired by the NCNW. The first floor was used as a reception and conference area, utilizing the original parlor and other rooms. The second story contained the NCNW offices and Bethune's residence, while the third floor was redecorated and fitted out

Window hood and roof cornice both characteristic of the Italianate style.

Front elevation.

Facade seen as part of a row of Italianate houses.

with a kitchenette. Nonetheless, the building still preserves many characteristics of a speculatively built rowhouse from the last quarter of the nineteenth century. The first floor retains its double parlors which are mirrored on the second story by two large bedrooms. Detailing at the stairway and around the door and window openings is largely original, including the pocket doors between the two parlors. The exterior of the house preserves its heavy window and door lintels.

After a fire in 1966, the NCNW established a new headquarters on Connecticut Avenue in the Dupont Circle neighborhood. In 1975 the organization began restoring the Bethune House and in 1979 established the Mary McLeod Bethune Museum and Archives which continue to occupy the building. The rehabilitation of the Bethune House has accompanied the redevelopment of the neighborhood in recent decades.

Stair hall.

Front parlor.

Bedroom with fireplace surround in white marble,
typical of an Italianate townhouse.

Jacob Christopher House

St. Louis, Missouri

Jacob Christopher, the builder of this house, was just one of many prominent residents of the Lafayette Park area of St. Louis during the last quarter of the nineteenth century. President of the Christopher & Simpson Architectural Iron and Foundry Company from 1882, Christopher was born near Strasbourg, France, and later immigrated to the United States, settling in St. Louis in 1850. Christopher's association with W. S. Simpson began in 1873; he had married Simpson's sister Harriet in 1858. Among the many applications of architectural iron suggested by *The Manufacturer and Builder* magazine in 1878 were the "iron crestings and finials of French or mansard roofs." Although such iron elements do not survive on Christopher's impressive house, it does display the steeply pitched Mansard roof associated with the French Second Empire style. The use of that architectural idiom — associated with additions to the Louvre Museum and other grand projects undertaken by the Second Empire of Napoléon III — signaled Christopher's economic, social, and architectural ambitions.

Lafayette Park was laid out in 1836 and is the oldest park in St. Louis as well as the first park west of the Mississippi River. Thirty acres in size, it was named for the French General Lafayette, a supporter of the American Revolution who visited St. Louis as part of a triumphant tour of the United States in 1825. This made Christopher's selection all the more appropriate. While it became a fashionable residential enclave later in the century, at the time of its creation, Lafayette Park was too remote from the city's center to be a viable area in which to live. For years it was known as "Grimsley's Folly" for Colonel Thornton Grimsley, a member of the Board of Aldermen, who had supported the project. Although St. Louis's population could not initially support the city's expansion towards Lafayette Park, it grew by nine times between 1840 and 1860. Thereafter, Lafayette Park became desirable both as a place to live near and as a recreation spot.

The houses surrounding Lafayette Park represent most of the predominant architectural styles of the second half of the nineteenth century — the French Second Empire, Italianate, Queen Anne — and a variety of alternatives in urban residential building. Included in the surrounding area are rowhouses, large freestanding residences, and houses like the Christopher House that, although separated from their neighbors, are deliberately positioned in close proximity to them. The houses in the Lafayette Park area substantiate architect John Wellborn Root's statement, made in 1893, that "It may be prophesied with certainty that, as a result of the architectural movement now in progress, Western cities like Chicago, St. Louis, Kansas City, Minneapolis, Milwaukee, and many others will, within a short time, present streets unrivalled in the world for variety, picturesqueness, and beauty of their domestic architecture."

The building's facade is emphasized by the use of stone. In light of the proximity of his house to his neighbors, Christopher left the side elevations in red brick. Characteristic of the Second Empire style are the molded window and door surrounds on the front of the house. The wide cornice supported by paired brackets is also a feature of the Second Empire style. The most immediately noticeable feature of the Christopher House is its scale. Windows on the first floor of the facade are between ten and eleven feet in height, reflecting the high ceilings at that level. While the proportions of the house are exceptionally tall, its essentials are those of smaller-scale rowhouses from earlier in the century. The facade is three bays wide and there is a side entrance.

A distinction between the plan of this house and those of many earlier rowhouses is the extension into the lot. The principal mass of the house that fronts on the street was originally given over to a large double parlor; the two rooms were subsequently combined into one longer living room with two hearths against the exterior wall. Behind this main block extended another section with a dining room and kitchen with

View showing stone used at the front facade and brick exposed at the side, as well as the Mansard roof.

Entrance hall with stair.

pantries beyond. Although the functions of these rooms have shifted in response to modern requirements, their original dimensions have been preserved. The interior finishes are characteristic of the last quarter of the nineteenth century: dark-stained, heavily turned decorative elements are combined with wide plaster moldings at the ceilings and marble fireplace surrounds. The finishes are somewhat less elaborate at the second floor, where the original layout of the double parlors and dining room is reflected in the arrangement of the three bedrooms directly over them.

Like many other areas within the city of St. Louis, Lafayette Square deteriorated around the time of the Great Depression. Nonetheless, enthusiasm for its exceptional architectural character remained and in 1972 the city made Lafayette Square its first historic district. In subsequent decades many houses in the area, like the Jacob Christopher House, have been renovated by private owners.

View of living area in parlor.

Modernized kitchen.

Dining area in parlor.

Bedroom.

Modernized bathroom.

Knabe House

Baltimore, Maryland

The Knabe House, whose nineteenth-century owners were associated with a prominent Baltimore piano factory, is in one of the city's many neighborhoods that are defined by their rowhouses. From the eighteenth century onward, Baltimore's rows grew from its busy port and climbed up and down its hills. The rowhouse became one of the types most closely associated with Baltimore. This is an example of the rowhouse built for well-off Baltimoreans, in a style that represents the turn away from the Italianate brownstone after 1875.

The Knabe Piano Company was started in 1833 in Baltimore by Wilhelm Knabe, who was born and educated in Germany. He began in partnership with Henry Gaehle under the name of Knabe & Gaehle, which lasted until 1854. Knabe's death ten years later has been attributed to the stress he endured during the economically slack period of the Civil War. After his demise, Knabe's sons William and Ernest took over the business and expanded it to New York and Washington. Knabe pianos became renowned musical instruments, favored by such virtuosi as Camille Saint-Saens. A Knabe piano was purchased for the Executive Mansion of Maryland around 1870. By the 1880s, the Knabe Piano Company was one of the largest employers in Baltimore.

At this moment, the population of Baltimore was swelling, from around 332,000 in 1880 to more than a half-million in 1890. Many of the newcomers came for manufacturing jobs. During the same decade, the number of manufacturers in the city rose by forty percent. Despite the population increase, Baltimore did not resort to apartment construction; the city saw itself as a "city of homes," in which a broad range in the size and cost of rowhouses fit all people.[1] At the turn of the century one commentator observed the dearth of tenements in Baltimore: "For happy Baltimore brooks not these plague-spots upon our boasted civilization."

The purchase of this house in the 1890s, shortly after its construction, by the Knabe family, reflects a period of prosperity for Baltimore's manufacturers. It was also a time when the regularity of earlier Italianate rowhouses, predominant in such neighborhoods as Bolton Hill, were coming to be considered visually boring. The building out of the Mount Vernon neighborhood offered an opportunity to explore a diversity of architectural styles. As the *Baltimore Sun* observed in 1878, "The variety and style to be observed in the erection of the dwellings is sufficient to avoid the monotony of unbroken similarity, which is so painfully apparent in some otherwise beautiful sections of the city." By 1896 *Harper's* called the neighborhood that extended outward from Mount Vernon Square "the most fashionable residential quarter of Baltimore."

Mount Vernon's fashionability derived, at least in part, from its architectural diversity, as *Harper's* pointed out. The Knabe House facade embodies the variety of materials that Mount Vernon houses represented. While constructed of red brick, a material that had been used for Baltimore rowhouses since the eighteenth century, the first story of the Knabe House is clad in brownstone. The material is used to accentuate the entrance level, to distinguish the house from the purely brick residences seen elsewhere in the city, and match it with the adjacent houses. The brownstone is brought forward slightly and the openings in it are delicately molded. The actual asymmetry of the four-bay facade is visually counteracted by the large arched window to the left of the front door.

Inside, the Knabe House reflects the reconsideration of the rowhouse type that had taken place by the 1880s and a major renovation of the original house by the Knabes. Gone is the Italianate side hall; instead there is a paneled living hall from which the parlor extends toward the front of the house and the dining room toward the rear. Flanking the entrance is a small study. The most astonishing part of the interior, however, is the room which was added to the rear of the house. Although it now serves as the kitchen, it was originally a kind of indoor garden, supported at either side by rows of monolithic marble columns. Period photographs document the presence along the sides of the room of extensive planters and lush foliage, which gave the room its distinctive character.

1. Mary Ellen Hayward and Charles Belfoure, *The Baltimore Rowhouse* (New York: Princeton Architectural Press, 1999).

ca. 1880 ■

Facade detail showing brownstone used at the first story.

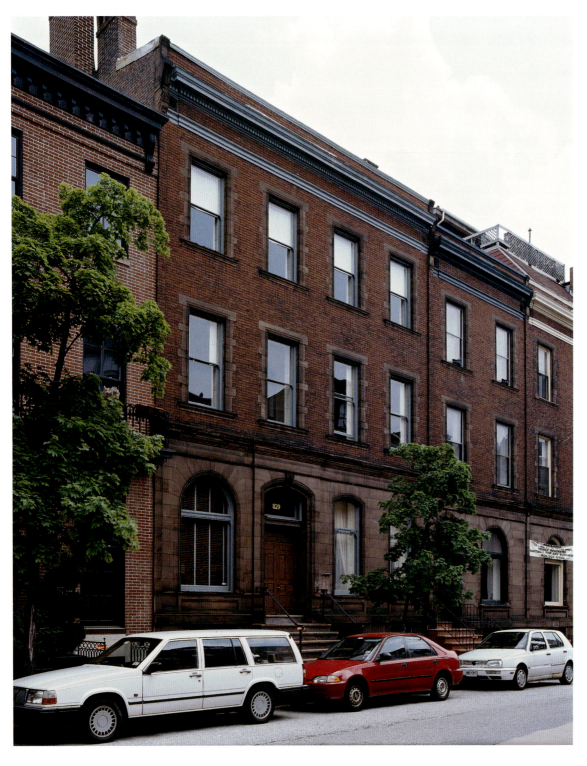

Street facade with adjoining houses.

Front parlor.

Paneled dining room.

Marble columns in the modernized kitchen.

View into kitchen at rear, formerly a garden room.

Modernized bathroom.

Bedroom with bed recessed into arched niche.

William Kehoe House

Savannah, Georgia

A native of County Wexford, Ireland, William Kehoe came to Savannah as a child. He apprenticed as an iron molder and then went on to prosper as the owner of an iron foundry. In the 1880s, when Kehoe built his house, Savannah was growing rapidly as a commercial and manufacturing center; the city's iron foundries consumed 200 tons of pig-iron per year. Despite its growth and modernization after the Civil War, I. W. Avery observed in *Harper's* in 1888 that, "No city of the Union blends more palpably the old and the new than Savannah…The past is a living presence in this beautiful old city." Kehoe's house fit Avery's description.

Like earlier Savannah townhouses, the Kehoe House is three bays wide on its entrance front, although its corner site allows one of the longer side elevations to be exposed and opened with windows. The dimensions of those openings are all long in accordance with the Italianate style. The second, parlor level has the longest windows and contains the main entrance which is accessed by a row of steps leading to a front porch above a raised basement. Exterior detailing in the Italianate style includes iron balconies that wrap around the parlor level and the level above it. Such balconies are features of Savannah's domestic architecture of the nineteenth century.

Inside, the Kehoe House is built on a well-known rowhouse plan. The side stairhall, at the parlor floor, provides access to two adjoining reception rooms that could be separated by sliding doors. The moldings are boldly scaled, consistent with the date of the house, and there are many common decorative features, including pier mirrors and plaster ceiling medallions. There is a vertical hierarchy of spaces,

the scales of the rooms and the elaborateness of their finishes diminishing as one moves up through the three stories.

William Kehoe and his wife Annie had ten children. To accommodate his family, in 1892 Kehoe built a larger house in Savannah overlooking Columbia Square. The Kehoes' later house was fully freestanding but like the earlier one, incorporated much iron detailing on the exterior, perhaps as a symbol of the industry in which William Kehoe had made his fortune.

Shadow cast on front steps by the iron railing.

1883 ▪

Front elevation.

View through double parlors.

Stair hall.

Bedroom.

Stair hall at upper level.

Dining room.

Queen Anne and Other Revivals

Ballantine House

Newark, New Jersey
George Edward Harney, Architect

The Ballantine House preserves a lavishly appointed domestic environment of the Victorian era. It also represents a certain type of urban house: originally freestanding, it stood quite close to the neighboring buildings. They formed a unified sequence of residences fronting on Newark's Washington Park.

At this time, Newark was in the midst of an enormous expansion. The city's population had grown from about 17,000 in 1840 to more than 105,000 in 1870. In 1877 it was ranked "the third city of the Union in manufacturing importance." Among the industries that attracted a diverse working-class population, including many immigrants, were the breweries. The Ballantine was the largest of the "Big Five" Newark breweries by the late 1870s.

John Holme Ballantine, whose family's brewery created the wealth that built the house, became president of the corporation following the death of its founder Peter Ballantine (John Holme Ballantine's grandfather) in 1883. The younger Ballantine would fill the position until his death in 1895. As historian Ulysses Grant Dietz notes, once John Ballantine became president of the family business, "he immediately began plans for a townhouse suitable to his new position." In 1879 Ballantine moved with his wife, Jeannette Boyd, and their four children to 43 Washington Street, opposite Washington Park. Then he purchased the house at 47 Washington Street and demolished both to make way for his new house. The house that Ballantine had architect George Edward Harney (1840–1924) design would blend with his brother Robert's adjacent house and with the eighteenth-century Marcus L. Ward House on the other side, as is demonstrated by an 1892 view of the three buildings.

Ballatine's requirements included not only a fancy house befitting his position, but also an elaborate stable at the rear of the property. Perhaps he was drawn to the architect by Harney's expertise with outbuildings as well as with residential work. Harney had a private architectural practice that he operated out of offices in Cold Spring and Newburgh, New York, in the Hudson Valley from 1863 on. He also distributed his designs through publications, such as *New York Horticulturalist* and *New England Farmer* magazines. His plan book, *Barns, Outbuildings and Fences*, was published in 1870.

The interior arrangement of the Ballantine House is a type in common use since the eighteenth century, the Georgian plan. There is a central stair hall which at the first story provides access to a wide variety of rooms reflecting the scale of the house as well as a Victorian nomenclature. On the south side of the hall, as Dietz points out, Harney created a suite of private rooms for daily use, consisting of a library, dining room, and music room. On the north side were the more public reception room and parlor, which would have been reserved for entertaining. At the second story were four bedrooms, as well as a boudoir above the front entrance, and servants' rooms to the rear above the first-floor billiard room. The third floor originally contained five main rooms, which were likely used as bedrooms and sitting rooms for the Ballantine's children. A large library or living room was added to the rear of this level in 1899 when a daughter, Alice, married and took up residence in the house.

Detail of entrance porch showing neoclassical elements executed in stone to contrast with the brick walls.

Facade overlooking Washington Park.

Streetscape view with Ballantine House at left.

The interior treatment, with its fine woodwork and rich finishes, resulted from two decorating projects. At the time of the original construction, the Ballantines hired the New York decorating firm of D.S. Hess & Co. to fit out the interior. Not long after, in 1891, "a major redecoration was undertaken of the entrance hall, reception room, parlor and music room," led by Roux & Co., another New York firm. The redecoration reflected changing use of the house by the maturing Ballantine family, and it was also a bid to remain fashionable, particularly when tastes were changing quickly.

Although certain modifications had been made to the house in order to accommodate Alice Ballantine and her family, the residence was sold to the Commercial Casualty Insurance Company after the death of her parents in 1919. By World War I, Washington Park was losing its residential character and becoming a commercial center. Despite its use as a place of business, few changes were made to the house. It was acquired by the Newark Museum Association in 1937, which had constructed a building on the site of the Ward House in 1925. The Newark Museum subsequently restored the Ballantine House and continues to operate it as part of the museum.[1]

The exterior of the Ballantine House has largely retained its original appearance. The symmetrical masonry facade with a blend of Renaissance and Gothic details suggests a moment in the history of Washington Park when it was bordered by ambitious urban residences.

1. Ulysses Grant Dietz, *The Ballantine House and the Decorative Arts Galleries at the Newark Museum* (Newark, New Jersey: The Newark Museum, 1994).

Third-floor library, or living room.

Parlor in the French style — considered modern in 1885.
The ceiling treatment was simplified in 1891.

Library with its original "old red" color — restored
in 1976 with gold leaf decoration.

Hallway at first floor.

Master bedroom shared by John and Jeanette Ballantine.

John Jacob Glessner House

Chicago, Illinois
Henry Hobson Richardson, Architect

In 1893 John Wellborn Root could look back on two decades of change in Chicago architecture, particularly in the design of urban houses. In part, the transformations were due to the Great Chicago Fire of 1871, which led to proscriptions against the use of wood that had been prevalent. They were also the result of architect H. H. Richardson's (1838–1886) example. Born in the South and trained at Harvard as well as at the École des Beaux-Arts in Paris, Richardson's practice was initially based in New York and later in Brookline, Massachusetts. He played an important role in American architecture by inspiring a revival of Romanesque French and Spanish architecture. "Of course," wrote Root, Chicago and other Midwest and West-Coast cities "took 'Queen Anne' fever with alarming intensity;" however, "H. H. Richardson was one of the most efficient physicians in working the cure, for under his influence such architects as had been following Norman Shaw (blindly and ignorantly, as they had followed him) turned from him and began to follow the American." While the Glessner House did not spawn legions of imitations, it was part of the legacy of Richardson's architecture, which did have a profound impact in Chicago and elsewhere.

Before the Chicago Fire, Root maintained, the city's houses had been "in general arrangement not unlike the corresponding house in New York," with high stoop entrances, side halls "separated from the entrance only by space for the hat-tree," and double parlors. The exteriors, however, often sported florid decoration making "the street aspects of such houses" seem comparatively "gayer and less solid." But solidity was what the Glessner House was all about. As architect and historian Thomas C. Hubka wrote, "The Glessner House represented a radical departure, even from the robust norm of late-nineteenth century Victorian eclecticism" by doing away with the usual trappings of domestic architecture of the period, including large windows, porches, and familiar decorative details. Rather, Richardson created a contrast between the fortress-like facades along Prairie Avenue and Eighteenth Street, and the more open elevations

that gave onto the interior courtyard formed by the house's L-shaped plan.

The house was constructed on three lots which had been subdivided for standard-width attached Chicago houses. The property was purchased by John Jacob Glessner in 1885 who recognized that even by combining the three lots, he would still not be able to build a freestanding house of the size of the other large residences on the street, while allowing for open space around the structure. Thus Richardson planned to attach the house to the adjoining one further south on Prairie Avenue, although it had not yet been constructed. In this way he was able to wrap the Glessner House around the corner of Prairie Avenue and Eighteenth Street, using the building itself to form a barrier between the public ways and the interior of the property. This arrangement had the added benefit of addressing the colder north and east sides (along Eighteenth Street and Prairie Avenue, respectively) with a relatively solid wall, and opening the house to the south with windows onto the courtyard. Although the basic arrangement of the house proved Richardson's brilliance as a planner, the design was met with a mixture of incomprehension and revulsion by the neighborhood which was thrown "into a state of stupefaction" according to the *Chicago Evening Journal*.

As Hubka has shown, Richardson relied on a number of historical sources in planning and designing the elevations of the Glessner House. The plan itself seems to have been inspired by a plan for a city house published in 1863 by the French medievalist architect E. E. Viollet-le-Duc, and it is known that the client gave Richardson an admired view of the medieval abbey at Abingdon, England, to which the architect made reference in developing the design. The medieval inspiration is apparent in the fortress-like exteriors of the Prairie Avenue and Eighteenth Street facades, and in the variety of towers and projections on the courtyard elevations which recall a fortified castle or town. Characteristic of Richardson's work is the use of rough, rock-faced stone on the public elevations where overscaled arches mark the entrances.[1]

1. Thomas C. Hubka, "H. H. Richardson's Glessner House: A Garden in the Machine," *Winterthur Portfolio* 24, no. 4 (Winter 1989): 209–229.

1887

Entrance detail.

Prairie Avenue facade. In his 1923 Story of a House, *Glessner wrote that, "when first built, the house was subject of much remark by passersby."*

Although the plan of the Glessner House may have been related to the work of Viollet-le-Duc, it was a radical departure from the designs of earlier attached houses in Chicago or even from other large freestanding residences. Certainly, the rectangular portion of the house that was pushed up to Prairie Avenue recalled earlier, even Colonial, houses in that it had a center entrance with a pair of windows at either side (leaving aside the courtyard entrance passage that abutted the adjoining house to the south). The entrance, however, led to a kind of living hall which projected into the courtyard with a windowed bow. To the south of the entrance was the master bedroom and to the north (at the corner of Prairie Avenue and Eighteenth Street) was the library. Beyond this point, the plan proceeded in an unorthodox manner, with a long hallway strung along the north (Eighteenth Street) wall, giving access to a series of rooms that generally diminished in importance and public use from the living room to the service areas at the end of the chain that adjoins the carriage house at the far northwest corner of the property.

The interior treatment of the house represents Richardson's very personal interpretation of the Arts and Crafts domestic interior. Certain elements of the late-nineteenth-century home, inspired by English medieval revival, are in place, for example, beamed ceilings and paneled walls. However, Richardson adapts these, by simplifying and making more coherent what were seen as the overly decorative, fussy features of the late-Victorian interior.

With the construction of his house, John Jacob Glessner became a resident of a neighborhood that boasted many successful Chicagoans. Glessner was born in Zanesville, Ohio, and in 1864 became involved in the manufacturing of harvesting machinery as a member of the firm of Warder, Bushnell & Glessner in Springfield, Ohio. In 1870, the same year in which he married Frances Macbeth, Glessner moved to Chicago to promote the business and eventually helped merge his company with the International Harvester Company, of which he became a director. The house Glessner built for his family was a bold architectural statement, which went beyond an expression of wealth and status to suggest his far-sighted patronage of one of the most highly regarded American architects of the nineteenth century.

Courtyard.

Stair hall.

Interior view showing beamed ceilings and prevalent woodwork, both reflecting the interest in the Arts and Crafts movement shared by the architect and his clients.

Library.

Dining room.

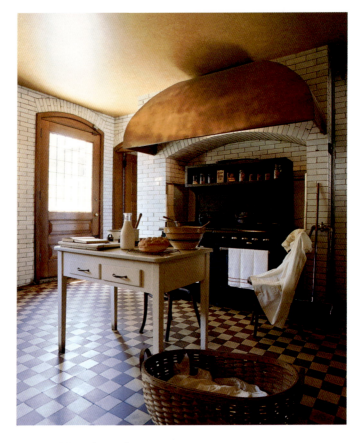

Kitchen with cast-iron cookstove.

Parlor.

William De Forest, Jr. House

New York City
William E. Mowbray, Architect

This rowhouse demonstrates the changes the type underwent as the residential development of Manhattan pushed northward during the last quarter of the nineteenth century. Although rowhouse construction had taken place in Harlem as early as the 1820s, it was during the last quarter of the nineteenth century that residences were constructed with intensity. These rowhouses were marketed to members of the middle class who commuted to work further south in Manhattan.

The house stands on part of the property that formerly went with Alexander Hamilton's fine Federal-period house, Hamilton Grange (1802), which was moved to another location in 1889. Ten years prior, the thirty-three-acre property had been purchased by a contractor named Anthony Mowbray who then sold it to William H. De Forest, a silk merchant and real estate investor, and his son. In the mid-1880s, the two capitalized on the introduction of a cable car railway on what is now Amsterdam Avenue. William De Forest, Jr., following his father's death, commissioned Anthony Mowbray's son, the architect William E. Mowbray, to design a group of eight houses (of which this is one) for a site on West 144th Street on the former Hamilton Grange property. The younger De Forest was living on the block by 1891.

As the *Real Estate Record and Builders' Guide* observed at the moment of completion, the houses represented a deliberate rejection of the monotony associated with prevailing rowhouse types: "It's evidently been a point with the improvers of Hamilton Grange that the old-time plain brown stone front should not find a place" in the newly developed neighborhood.[1] Rather, the houses were treated individually. Both the materials used and the historic styles referred to varied from house to house. With his family connection to Harlem's contractors and developers, Mowbray developed a successful practice in rowhouse design. The architect's ability to deliver residential designs that were imposing yet distinct from one another fit well with the requirements of the patron, as suggested by the restrictions the elder De Forest placed on the Hamilton Grange properties in 1886. The restrictive covenant he created in that year limited future construction in the neighborhood to "brick or stone dwelling houses at least two stories in height." De Forest had thus anticipated a range of materials being used for substantial houses. Not that he built rowhouses exclusively: Single-family residences, mostly three stories in height, were built along the numbered streets, Convent Avenue, and Hamilton Terrace, but a row of apartment buildings, most six-stories high, were constructed on the east side of Amsterdam Avenue between West 140th and West 145th Street. The De Forests relied on the same architect to do all of the buildings — apartment buildings and rowhouses — on a block to ensure the comprehensive treatment of the street facade.

1. Michael Henry Adams, *Harlem Lost and Found: An Architectural and Social History, 1765–1915* (New York: The Monacelli Press, 2002), 74–96.

Gable detail.

1890 ◉

Front elevation.

Entrance.

At the time of this row's completion, the press considered it to be "Gothic" in style. In fact, the houses reflected a variety of medieval architectural styles, ranging from the Gothic to the Romanesque and Tudor idioms, the last of which is seen in this building. The house corresponds to the client's desire for a combination of materials; random ashlar at the first story and yellow brick above. Tudor in inspiration are the stone mullions that frame the windows on the facade. The proportions of these are quite tall, reflecting the particular problem the architect addressed in squeezing an ambitious house onto a narrow lot. In keeping with many rowhouses in Harlem, the front entrance is reached by a long flight of steps.

Inside, the house reflects criticisms of the rowhouse plan since the Civil War. In particular, the arrangement of the parlor floor with a generous living hall and open staircase at the center shows the degree to which the affluent had turned away from the sidehall rowhouse, with its cramped vestibule and narrow stair. As the critic Marianna Griswold Van Rensselaer wrote in *The Century* (Nov. 1885–Apr. 1886), "If anything could be stupider than our old average exterior, it was certainly our old average interior." Prior to what she saw as the recent rethinking of the rowhouse interior, designers had done nothing more than "to make the narrowest possible dark hall with the narrowest impossible staircase, and to put three equal-sized rooms one behind the other." Variety in the shapes of rooms in this house is achieved in several ways, including through the projection of a three-sided bay off the rear wall. Various woods are also used throughout the interior, including for the elaborately detailed mantelpieces.

As architectural historian Michael Henry Adams claims, the De Forests' development scheme for Hamilton Heights was only partially successful. The elder De Forest was driven practically insane by his obligations to the speculative development and through the mid-1890s large swaths of the Hamilton Grange area were vacant lots. The market for rowhouses in the area was weak and builders awaited the expiration of De Forest's deed restrictions to construct apartment houses on the sites.

Stair hall.

Parlor.

Dining room.

Modernized bathroom.

opposite, top: One of many decorative mantelpieces in the house.

opposite, bottom: Bedroom.

Payne and Helen Hay Whitney House

New York City
McKim, Mead & White, Architects

This house is representative of changing architectural tastes at the turn of the century, particularly the rise of a decorative neoclassicism practiced by the premier firm of architects in New York. The Payne and Helen Hay Whitney House also epitomizes the custom-designed and built townhouse on Manhattan's most fashionable street: Fifth Avenue.

The architects hired by the Whitneys to build their house, a wedding gift from Colonel Oliver Hazard Payne to his nephew, were Charles Follen McKim (1847–1909), William Rutherford Mead (1846–1928), and Stanford White (1853–1906). Although the architects executed all manner of public and private commissions, it was White who was most closely connected to the fine residential work for which the firm was known. White's celebrated murder by Harry Thaw, the husband of his lover Evelyn Nesbit Thaw, in 1906, further delayed the construction of the Whitney House, which lasted for more than a half-dozen years.

Critic Russell Sturgis, writing in 1893, considered a custom designed townhouse to be an anomaly in New York: "In Boston, the man of some means, who wishes to have a house, employs an architect whom he considers the most intelligent or the most agreeable, and builds his house; in New York, the man, even of wealth, goes with his wife to look at ready-made houses, and accepts, buys, and pays for the one which is the least objectionable." By the end of this long process, Helen Hay Whitney felt it would have been easier to have bought an existing house: she wrote to Stanford White in 1906 after having heard from her mother that no recent progress had been made on the house that, "It made me so disgusted I felt like chucking the whole thing and getting a nice ready made house that I could have when I wanted it."

Despite such frustrations, the Whitneys must have been pleased with the results. Located at 972 Fifth Avenue, the house enjoyed a prestigious location near the Metropolitan Museum of Art, the neoclassical facade of which was completed just as the Whitneys were beginning their building project. The adjoining Henry Cook Townhouse, at 973 Fifth Avenue, was also designed by Stanford White and erected at the same time as the Whitney House. The front elevations of the two houses are treated as virtually a single composition, unified by the classical pilasters and engaged columns, although the Whitney House is distinguished by its swelled contour. While White's townhouse designs were restrained by his neoclassicism, the surrounding streets, built out around the turn of the century, featured a wide variety of historicist residences, some quite florid and ostentatious. The light stone front of the Whitney House reflected turn-of-the-century tastes, which had turned against late-nineteenth-century brick and brownstone. The use of Corinthian pilasters to articulate the bays of the upper stories of the curved facade would also have signaled the fashionable nature of the design.

Entrance detail.

1902–9 ✦

Fifth Avenue facade.

1. Jeni Sandberg, "Stanford White's House for Payne Whitney in New York City," *The Magazine Antiques* Vol. CLXII, No. 4 (Oct., 2002): 122–9.

At the ground level, the house turned a relatively austere face to Fifth Avenue with a rusticated stone wall pierced by small windows flanking the central door. The domed entrance hall, with a fountain at the center supported by paired marble columns, was something of a surprise, although its plan echoed the curve of the house's facade. Adjacent to the entrance hall, the "Venetian" reception room offered another contrasting spatial and visual experience. The room was entirely mirrored and originally filled with European furnishings. When the house was sold out of the Whitney family in 1949, the room was dismantled and stored on Long Island until it was reinstalled in 1997 by the current occupants, the Cultural Services Office of the French Embassy. Such elaborate interiors required the work of many New York decorators and craftspeople, as historian Jeni Sandberg has demonstrated. For example, the second-story salon was executed by Jules Allard et Fils, a French firm that required legions of designers, carpenters, and ornamentalists to complete. The room's furnishings were mostly purchased by White in Europe.[1]

Payne Whitney came from a wealthy and politically and socially well-connected family and was educated at Yale College and Harvard Law School. He was a successful financier and businessman as well as a horse racing enthusiast. Following his death at his Long Island estate in 1927, Whitney's wife maintained the Fifth Avenue residence until her own death in 1944. Like Payne, Helen Hay Whitney had come from a political family; her father John Hay had been President Abraham Lincoln's secretary and had served as Ambassador to Great Britain and in other diplomatic and government posts. The house was acquired by the French government in 1952.

Detail of upper level of facade.

Entrance hall with stair.

Entrance hall with fountain and a male figure
attributed to Michelangelo Buonarroti.

Stair hall at second story.

Venetian reception room.

John Ryan House

San Francisco, California
Andrew Mann, Architect (2001 Addition)

"[T]here is in Western cities a notable absence, compared with cities in the East, of houses built in blocks." While architect John W. Root attributed this phenomenon, in 1893, to the relative availability of land in the West, in fact some Western cities — like San Francisco — had attached, semi-detached, and completely detached urban houses as a result of high land values. The Ryan House, while recently expanded, typifies the kind of tightly packed development of neighborhoods of modest detached houses, which characterized much of San Francisco beginning in the second half of the nineteenth century.

Although San Francisco possesses more areas of detached houses than do many Eastern cities, this is not due to the availability of substantially larger lots. Many of the city's neighborhoods were divided into lots varying in width from twenty-five to thirty feet. They were thus wider than the common twenty-foot lots of the East Coast, but far narrower than a sub-urban lot that would accommodate a large house ringed with lawn and plantings. San Francisco lots were often as deep as 137 feet. The house commonly erected on an urban lot in San Francisco was a balloon-frame "predesigned 'box' onto which many additions and adornments could be grafted to suit individual needs and tastes." Deep but narrow, such houses gathered most of their details to the short street elevations. Typically, the houses had side stair halls with two to five rooms strung along them, one behind the other, with their sizes and importance diminishing toward the back.[1]

Several common varieties were developed in San Francisco to take advantage of available lots and to accommodate its hilly topography. Among the variations was the single-story artisan cottage, the type originally represented by the Ryan House. In this instance, the house was built on a raised base that evened off the sloping site. A flight of steps leads to the front entrance, which is located to the side of the gabled facade. The three-sided bay, projecting from the facade, reflects the location of the parlor, which

had a larger room behind it that opened onto smaller bedrooms and a kitchen at the rear. As is common for detached houses in San Francisco, the Ryan House stands very close to its neighbors at either side, thus window openings in the front and back are maximized to increase light and ventilation. Despite its small size, the house (even before its recent expansion) incorporated many of the decorative elements found on larger residences. In addition to the bay window, the front porch was supported by a turned column while the gable was finished in decorative shingles.

The original house was either built or owned by one John Ryan who authorized the connection of water service to the property in 1910. In raising the house to a full two stories, architect Andrew Mann retained the feeling of the original house. Without adding significantly to its footprint on the lot, the house has been nearly doubled in square-footage, making its size more in keeping with contemporary requirements. At the facade, the bay has been extended into the second story and its gable is finished

1. Anne Vernez Moudon, *Built for Change: Neighborhood Architecture in San Francisco* (Cambridge, MA and London: MIT Press, 1986).

Street facade before renovation and expansion.

Facade view showing typical San Francisco planning with narrow houses closely adjoining one another.

1908 ✸

with shingling in a decorative pattern. The Ryan House thus continues to contribute to what Root considered the architectural variety of West Coast cities: "In driving through [their] streets the eye is at no time wearied with the monotony which is so tiresome in Fifth Avenue or other similar streets in Eastern cities, but is everywhere delighted with constant change, constant appeal to new sentiment, and that delightful sense of the picturesque which, to the stranger, is so inspiriting."

Modernized kitchen.

opposite, top: Parlor looking into bay at front.

opposite, bottom: Dining room.

Hall lit by skylight.

Renovated bathroom.

Bedroom with facade bay at right.

George A. Didden House

Washington, D.C.
Clement August Didden and Son, Architects

The work of architects who had an important impact on Washington's domestic architecture, this house represents the late-nineteenth-century development of the Capitol Hill neighborhood. It is also marked by various historical design influences, including the Romanesque Revival — popular among many German-American architects — as well as the turn-of-the-century Neoclassical Revival.

The house represents the work of Clement August Didden (1837–1923), who was born and educated in Germany, following several generations of architects in his family. After practicing architecture in Germany, Didden moved to New York in 1866 where he worked for the firm of Fernbach, Hunt and Post. In the early 1870s Didden worked in Philadelphia with Fraser, Furness and Hewitt, in which the well-known Frank Furness was a principal. Following Fraser's departure for Washington, D.C., Furness and Hewitt reorganized the firm and sent Didden to Washington as their representative, a role he continued to play until 1876. Didden practiced architecture in Washington, D.C. until 1921, producing designs for many residential buildings that used decorative brick and historicist elements. He worked with his son, and together they formed the firm of C. A. Didden and Son, Architects. By the time of his father's retirement, George A. Didden (1876–unknown) was listed in official documents as a government clerk, so it is unclear how committed he was to architectural practice and what role he played in the firm he operated with his father. Although many of Clement August Didden's commissions were in Washington, D.C., he also designed houses in other major cities on the East Coast.

George A. Didden was married to Marie Carry Didden, the daughter of one of his father's business associates, Albert Carry, who was also a German immigrant and a successful businessman. Carry owned and ran the National Capital Brewing Company in Washington, and then Carry's Ice Cream Company during prohibition. C. A. Didden designed several buildings for Carry, including his house at the northwest corner of Twelfth and Independence Avenue on Capitol Hill. The house the younger Diddens occupied was built on property that was originally part of Carry's lot.

Although it is essentially a familiar two-and-a-half story, three-bay rowhouse, the Didden House stands out from its neighbors by virtue of its expertly handled facade details and rich color palette. Constructed of red brick, the facade has some contrasting brownstone trim elements. These include the entrance enframement, the keystones in the arches above the windows, and the projecting sills below the second-story windows. Some of the massive appearance of the Didden House comes from the brownstone railing, supported by squat posts, that wraps around the front stoop. The Palladian window at the first story represents contemporary interests in Renaissance classicism, while other details suggest the architects' engagement with the Romanesque Revival. The dormer especially, almost merged as it is into the slope of the tiled roof, recalls the work of H. H. Richardson, the nineteenth-century popularizer of the Romanesque.

Detail of brickwork and brownstone trim at entrance.

1910–11 ✸

Front elevation.

Stair hall.

The interior of the Didden House is spacious, demonstrating that this is an ample house in comparison to other rowhouses built in D.C. at the same time. It also illustrates the rethinking of the traditional rowhouse plan that had taken place by the time of its construction. At the center of the first floor is the large stairhall, very different from the cramped side hall that characterized earlier city houses or the smaller houses on Capitol Hill. Also inside is the dark wood trim that had been popular for house design since the last quarter of the nineteenth century. The hall has paneling below the staircase, adding to the impression of warm and comfortable domesticity.

The Didden House represents changing ideas of what an urban house should be and also reflects a period of growth for Capitol Hill, which began after the Civil War as the federal government expanded in size. With the passage of the Civil Service Reform Act of 1883, which put an end to the spoils system and made government employment more attractive,

View from hall to dining room.

Capitol Hill became an even more sought-after middle-class neighborhood. Although the financial downturn of 1893 slowed growth, at the time the Didden House was built, Capitol Hill was about to experience enormous expansion, between the first and second world wars when "the Hill's population swelled to the bursting point." This influx contributed to maintaining the neighborhood's diverse communities, accommodated in residences such as this one that were characterized by great architectural diversity.[1]

1. Ruth Ann Overbeck, "Capitol Hill: The Capitol is Just Up the Street" in *Washington At Home*, Kathryn Schneider Smith, ed., (Northridge, CA: Windsor Publications, Inc., 1988).

Front parlor.

Dining room.

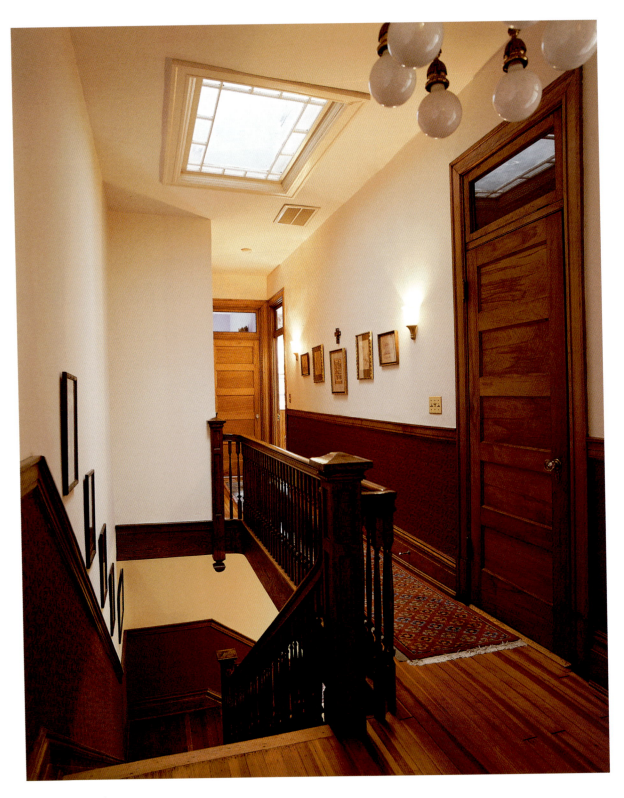

Stair hall at second story.

opposite, top: Bathroom.

opposite, bottom: Bedroom.

Glenn and Ida Moore House

Rancho Santa Fe, California

Requa and Jackson, Architects, with Lilian Rice

The town of Rancho Santa Fe is located on property acquired by the Atchison, Topeka & Santa Fe Railroad in 1906, some 106 acres of an earlier grant of nearly 9,000 acres made to Juan Osuna by the government of Mexico and subsequently known as Rancho San Dieguito. The railroad company intended to use the property to grow eucalyptus trees that could be harvested to produce railroad ties. The trees, however, were not suitable and the land was subsequently developed by the Santa Fe Land Improvement Company.[1] As architectural historian Will Chandler has documented, the Company hired L. G. Sinnard, who had laid out communities for the Southern Pacific Railway, to plan Rancho Santa Fe. At the center of the plan, Sinnard laid out the Paseo Delicias, a broad avenue with a center parkway that ran from the town entrance to the guesthouse. The original conception of Rancho Santa Fe was an anomaly in southern California, where growth was somewhat unplanned and decentralized. By contrast, Rancho Santa Fe had a traditional civic center with a blend of public, commercial, and residential uses. The group of townhouses, of which the Glenn and Ida Moore House is one, was an important part of that center.

The Santa Fe Land Improvement Company also brought in the architectural firm of Richard Requa and Herbert Jackson to plan the original buildings, including its own offices, the inn, gas station, and townhouses. Lilian Rice (1888–1938) was Richard Requa's project architect in Rancho Santa Fe, beginning in 1923, and has been credited with the designs of the townhouses. One of the first women to graduate from the School of Architecture at the University of California, Berkeley, in 1910, Rice opened her own office in Rancho Santa Fe in 1928.

Architect Richard Requa was likely responsible for the choice of style for the buildings of Rancho Santa Fe, the "Spanish Colonial" having been a popular idiom in California in the 1920s. The adobe and red terra cotta roof tiles that are hallmarks of the style were thought to evoke the architecture of the

southern Mediterranean that was adapted to a warm climate like California's and that had had an important cultural impact on the southwestern United States. In fact, the architecture of Rancho Santa Fe was initially not so much Spanish as Mexican, as Chandler points out: The adobe was painted mustard yellow and window trim bright turquoise blue. By the mid-1930s, however, the Mexican Pueblo style was ruled out by the Rancho Santa Fe building codes which thereafter specifically called for the use of a more Spanish or Mediterranean idiom for construction in the town.

Although the attached houses of Rancho Santa Fe were referred to as "townhouses" or "rowhouses," they shared little with other examples of those types. In fact, the houses were more like attached bungalows with walled patios. The interior of the Glenn and Ida Moore House is arranged like a modest detached house of the period, with a living room, dining room, and kitchen at the front, and a pair of bedrooms sharing a bath behind them. Wrought iron details and arched openings between interior rooms suggested a relationship to the Mexican adobe style.

Glenn Moore was the resident landscape designer and nurseryman of Rancho Santa Fe. As the plantings for his own house show, Moore created a lush density of plant materials in an environment that had previously been desert. The front yard of the house was planted with tree ferns and the back part of the property with four eucalyptus trees. From 1926 until the time of the Depression, Moore ran a successful landscaping business in Rancho Santa Fe, but the economic downturn forced him to seek work in La Jolla. Moore was manager of the Rancho Santa Fe Golf Course from 1940 to 1946, when he and Ida Moore divorced and he left the area. Ida Moore was postmistress of Rancho Santa Fe for a time and lived in the house until her death in 1982.

The project was seen as a way of achieving coherence and providing some of the amenities of a city in a rural development. As Lee Shipley wrote in

1. Meriam Ames et al., eds., *Rancho Santa Fe: A California Village* (Rancho Santa Fe, CA: Rancho Santa Fe Historical Society, 1993); Lilian J. Rice, "More Building in 1928 than Ever Before," *Rancho Santa Fe Progress* 1, no. 7 (January 1928): 11, 14.

Front facade.

1926

View towards the rear of the property where a two-story addition was made in 2004.

the *American City Magazine* in 1924, "The real aim of the Santa Fe […] was to work out a problem in rural life — to create a community which would demonstrate that rural life can be made more attractive than urban life." Key to that demonstration was the integration of uses that the Rancho Santa Fe village center provided. It is just that kind of interweaving of functions that enables residents to walk easily between their homes, schools, stores and workplaces, which is now being promoted by the New Urbanist movement.

Family room in the two-story addition.

Living room in the original front portion of the house.

opposite, top: Modern kitchen in the wing of the house that was added in 2004.

opposite, bottom: Modernized bathroom.

Bibliography

In addition to books, articles, and unpublished studies, important resources for the study of townhouses include the records of local and state historic preservation agencies, nominations to the National Register of Historic Places (for both historic districts and individual buildings), and the records of the Historic American Building Survey. The last can be obtained through the Web site of the Library of Congress.

Adams, Michael Henry. *Harlem, Lost and Found: An Architectural and Social History, 1765–1915*. New York: Monacelli Press, 2002.

Aidala, Thomas. *The Great Houses of San Francisco*. 2nd ed. New York: Arch Cape Press, 1987.

Alexander, Robert L. "Baltimore Row Houses of the Early Nineteenth Century." *American Studies* 16 (Fall 1975): 65–76.

Alexander, Robert. "The Riddell-Carroll House in Baltimore." *Winterthur Portfolio* 28, no. 2/3 (Summer 1993): 113–139.

Ames, Kenneth. "Robert Mills and the Philadelphia Row House." *Journal of the Society of Architectural Historians* 27, no. 2 (May 1968): 140–6.

Ames, Winslow. "New York Brownstones through German Eyes, 1851." *Journal of the Society of Architectural Historians* 25, no. 1 (Mar. 1966): 63–4.

Auchincloss, Louis. "The East Side Brownstone: A Cinderella Story." *Architectural Digest* 47, no. 12 (Nov. 1990): 35–40.

Ballon, Hilary. *The Paris of Henri IV: Architecture and Urbanism*. Cambridge, MA: MIT Press, c. 1991.

Binney, Marcus. *Town Houses: Urban Houses from 1200 to the Present Day*. New York: Whitney Library of Design, 1998.

Bunting, Bainbridge. *Houses of Boston's Back Bay, An Architectural History, 1840–1917*. Cambridge, MA: The Belknap Press of Harvard University Press, 1967.

Clark, Peter, ed. *The Early Modern Town*. London: Longman Group, 1976.

Clark Jr., Clifford. *The American Family Home, 1800–1960*. Chapel Hill: University of North Carolina Press, 1986.

Croly, Herbert. "The Renovation of the New York Brownstone District." *Architectural Record* 13 (June 1903): 55–71.

Downs, Arthur Channing Jr. "An Early Victorian Building Crane, and Hints on Building with Brownstone." *APT Journal* VII, no. 1 (1975): 87–8.

Elder, William Voss. *Robert Mills' Waterloo Row — Baltimore, 1816*. Baltimore: Baltimore Museum of Art, 1971.

Goodman, Phebe S. *The Garden Squares of Boston*. Hanover and London: University Press of New England, 2003.

Gorlin, Alexander. *The New American Town House*. New York: Rizzoli, 1999.

Hamlin, Talbot. *Greek Revival Architecture in America*. 1944. Reprint. New York: Dover, 1964.

Handlin, David P. *The American Home: Architecture and Society, 1815–1915*. Boston: Little Brown, 1979.

Hayward, Mary Ellen. "Urban Vernacular Architecture in Nineteenth-Century Baltimore." *Winterthur Portfolio* 16, no. 1 (Spring 1981): 33–63.

Hayward, Mary Ellen and Charles Belfoure. *The Baltimore Rowhouse*. New York: Princeton Architectural Press, 1999.

Herman, Bernard. *Town House: Architecture and Material Life in the Early American City, 1780–1830*. Chapel Hill: University of North Carolina Press for the Ohmohundro Institute for Early American History and Culture, 2005.

Heuer, Ann Rooney. *Town Houses*. New York: Friedman/Fairfax, 2000.

Huxtable, Ada Louise. *Classic New York*. Garden City, NY: Doubleday, 1964.

Kirker, Harold. *The Architecture of Charles Bulfinch*. Cambridge, MA: Harvard University Press, 1969.

Kitao, T. Kaori. "Philadelphia Row House." *Swarthmore College Bulletin*, April 1977, 6–11.

Lancaster, Clay. *Old Brooklyn Heights: New York's First Suburb*. Rutland, VT: C. E. Tuttle Co., 1961.

Landau, Sarah Bradford. "The Row Houses of New York's West Side." *Journal of the Society of Architectural Historians* 34, no. 1 (Mar. 1975): 19–36.

Lawrence, Henry W. "The Greening of the Squares of London: Transformation of Urban Landscapes and Ideals." *Annals of the Association of American Geographers*, 83, no. 1 (Mar. 1993): 90–118.

Lockwood, Charles. *Bricks and Brownstone, The New York Row House, 1783–1929*. 2nd ed. New York: Rizzoli, 2003.

Manbeck, John B., ed. *The Neighborhoods of Brooklyn*. 2nd ed. New Haven: Yale University Press, 2004.

Massey, James C. and Shirley Maxwell. "From Elegant Townhouse to Plain Rowhouse: The Party-Wall House." *Old-House Journal* 13, no. 7 (Aug.–Sept. 1985): 154–5.

Moss, Roger W. *Historic Houses of Philadelphia*. Philadelphia: University of Pennsylvania Press, 1998.

Moudon, Anne Vernez. *Built for Change: Neighborhood Architecture in San Francisco*. Cambridge, MA and London: MIT Press, 1986.

Murtagh, William John. "The Philadelphia Row House." *Journal of the Society of Architectural Historians* 16, no. 4 (Dec. 1957): 8–13.

Muthesius, Stefan. *The English Terraced House*. New Haven: Yale University Press, 1982.

Nonemaker, James A. "The New York Town House, 1815–1840." M.A. Thesis. University of Delaware, 1958.

Poesch, Jessie. *The Art of the Old South: Painting, Sculpture, Architecture & the Products of Craftsmen, 1560–1860*. New York: Knopf, 1983.

Seasholes, Nancy S. *Gaining Ground: A History of Landmaking in Boston*. Cambridge, MA and London: MIT Press, 2003.

Schuyler, Montgomery. "The Small City House in New York." *Architectural Record* 8 (Apr.–June 1899): 357–88.

Sennett, Richard. *The Conscience of the Eye*. New York: Knopf, 1990.

Shivers, Natalie W. *Those Old Placid Rows: The Aesthetic and Development of the Old Baltimore Rowhouse*. Baltimore: Maclay & Assoc., 1981.

Smith, Kathryn Schneider, ed. *Washington At Home*. Northridge, CA: Windsor Publications, Inc., 1988.

Smith, Margaret Supplee and John C. Moorehouse. "Architecture and the Housing Market: Nineteenth-Century Row Housing in Boston's South End." *Journal of the Society of Architectural Historians* 52, no. 2 (June 1993): 159–78.

Stevenson, Frederic R. and Carl Feiss. "Charleston and Savannah." *The Journal of the Society of Architectural Historians* 10, no. 4. (Dec. 1951): 3–9.

Stillman, Damie. "City Living, Federal Style." In *Everyday Life in the Early Republic*. Catherine E. Hutchins, ed. Winterthur, DE: H. F. Du Pont Winterthur Museum, 1984.

Sturgis, Russell et al. *Homes in the City and Country*. New York: Scribner's, 1893.

Tatum, George. *Philadelphia Georgian*. Middletown, CT: Wesleyan University Press, 1976.

Thomas, George E. "Architectural Patronage and Social Stratification in Philadelphia between 1840 and 1920." In *The Divided Metropolis: Social and Spatial Dimensions of Philadelphia, 1800–1975*, edited by William W. Cutler and Howard Gillette. Westport, CT: Greenwood Press, 1980.

VerPlanck, Christopher Patrick. "Building by the Book: John Cotter Pelton's 'Cheap Dwellings' of San Francisco, California 1880–1890." M.A. Thesis. University of Virginia, 1997.

Voorsanger, Catherine Hoover and John K. Howat, eds. *Art and the Empire City, New York, 1825–1861*. New York: Metropolitan Museum of Art; New Haven: Yale University Press, 2000.

Weinhardt, Jr., Carl J. "The Domestic Architecture of Beacon Hill, 1800–1850." *Proceedings of the Bostonian Society*, 1958, 11–32.

Wojtowicz, Robert, ed. *Sidewalk Critic: Lewis Mumford's Writings on New York*. New York: Princeton Architectural Press, 1998.

Wright, Gwendolyn. *Building the Dream: A Social History of Housing in America*. Cambridge, MA and London: MIT Press, 1981.

Zierden, Martha A. and Bernard L. Herman. "Charleston Townhouses: Archaeology, Architecture, and the Urban Landscape, 1750–1850." In *Landscape Archaeology: Reading and Interpreting the American Historical Landscape*, edited by Rebecca Yamin and Karen Bescherer Metheny. Knoxville: University of Tennessee Press, 1996, 193–227.

Ziskin, Rochelle. *The Place Vendôme: Architecture and Mobility in Eighteenth-Century Paris*. Cambridge, UK and New York: Cambridge University Press, 1999.

Credits

All photographs copyright © 2005 Radek Kurzaj, except the following.

p. 8: Scott A. Kuhagen, Photographer.

p. 11 (left): From *Maniere de Bastir pour Touttes Sortes de Personnes* (1623) by Pierre Le Muet.

pp. 11 (right), 12: Danielle Jansen, Photographer.

p. 13: Carrie Albee, Photographer.

p. 16 (bottom, left): Frank O. Branzetti, Photographer. Feb. 11, 1941. Historic American Buildings Survey, Library of Congress, Washington, D.C., HABS, MASS, 13-BOST, 26-1.

p. 16 (top): Walter Smalling, Jr., Photographer. July 1979. Historic American Buildings Survey, Library of Congress, Washington, D.C. HABS, MASS, 13-BOST, 26-9.

p. 16 (bottom, right): Walter Smalling, Jr., Photographer. July 1979. Historic American Buildings Survey, Library of Congress, Washington, D.C. HABS, MASS, 13-BOST, 26-4.

p. 17: Ernst Shütz, Photographer.

p. 18: E. H. Pickering, Photographer. July 1936. Historic American Buildings Survey, Library of Congress, Washington, D.C. HABS, MD, 4-BALT, 109-1.

p. 19 (top, left): E. H. Pickering, Photographer. June 1936. Historic American Buildings Survey, Library of Congress, Washington, D.C. HABS, MD, 4-BALT, 16-2.

p. 19 (top, right): Nineteenth-century photograph. Historic American Buildings Survey, Library of Congress, Washington, D.C. HABS, MD, 4-BALT, 16C-1.

p. 19 (bottom): E. H. Pickering, Photographer. August 1936. Historic American Buildings Survey, Library of Congress, Washington, D.C. HABS, MD, 4-BALT, 84-1.

pp. 1, 20 (left): Historic American Buildings Survey, Library of Congress, Washington, D.C. HABS, SC, 10-CHAR, 308-1.

p. 20 (right): Jack Landau, Photographer.

p. 21: Historic American Buildings Survey Drawing, Library of Congress, Washington, D.C. HABS, MASS, 13-BOST, 61-.

p. 22: Scott A. Kuhagen, Photographer.

p. 23 (top): E. P. MacFarland, Photographer. December 1935. Historic American Buildings Survey, Library of Congress, Washington, D.C., HABS, NY, 24-BROK, 35-2.

p. 23 (bottom): E. P. MacFarland, Photographer. December 1935. Historic American Buildings Survey, Library of Congress, Washington, D.C., HABS, NY, 24-BROK, 35-4.

p. 24 (top, left): E. P. MacFarland, Photographer. May 4, 1934. Historic American Buildings Survey, Library of Congress, Washington, D.C. HABS, NY, 31-NEYO, 18-1.

p. 24 (top, right): E. P. MacFarland, Photographer. May 4, 1934. Historic American Buildings Survey, Library of Congress, Washington, D.C. HABS, NY, 31-NEYO, 18-4.

p. 24 (bottom): E. P. MacFarland, Photographer. March 27, 1934. Historic American Buildings Survey, Library of Congress, Washington, D.C. HABS, NY, 31-NEYO, 12-1.

p. 25: Historic American Buildings Survey, Library of Congress, Washington, D.C. HABS, NY, 31-NEYO, 83-.

p. 27: Historic American Buildings Survey, Library of Congress, Washington, D.C. HABS, LA, 036-NEWOR, 105A-.

p. 28: From *The Second Treasury of Early American Homes* (1954) by Richard and Dorothy Pratt.

p. 29: E. H. Pickering, Photographer. September 1936. Historic American Buildings Survey, Library of Congress, Washington, D.C. HABS, MD, 4-BALT, 102-.

p. 29 (left): Historic American Buildings Survey, Library of Congress, Washington, D.C. HABS, MD, 4-BALT, 161-.

p. 29 (right): Historic American Buildings Survey, Library of Congress, Washington, D.C. HABS, MD, 4-BALT, 163-.

p. 31: www.waccorp.com.

p. 32 (top and bottom): Scott A. Kuhagen, Photographer.

p. 35 (top and bottom): Reprinted from Thomas Aidala, *Great Houses of San Francisco* (1987). Photograph by Curt Brace.

p. 36 (left): Reprinted from *American Architect and Building News* (1879).

p. 36 (right): Reprinted from T.H. Robsjohn-Gibbings, *Good-bye, Mr. Chippendale* (1944).

p. 38 (top, left): Historic American Buildings Survey, Library of Congress, Washington, D.C. HABS, MASS, 13-BOST, 112-1.

p. 38 (top, right): Historic American Buildings Survey, Library of Congress, Washington, D.C. HABS, MASS, 13-BOST, 112-2.

p. 38 (bottom): Ronald C. Saari, Photographer.

p. 40 (left and right): Reprinted from *House and Garden* magazine (December 1934).

p. 42 (top and bottom): Reprinted from *Southern Living* magazine (May 1972).

p. 43: Courtesy of Swarthmore College Publications Department.

p. 45 (top and bottom): Abby Aldrich Rockefeller Folk Art Museum, Colonial Williamsburg Foundation, Williamsburg, VA.

p. 98: Stan Ries, Photographer.

pp. 128–129: The National Parks Service.

p. 188: The Newark Museum.

p. 217: Andrew Mann, Architect.

pp. 230–235: Courtesy of Mark Benjamin. Reed Keastner, Photographer.

Index